D1432331

Five festal garments

Titles in this series:

1 *Possessed by God*, David Peterson
2 *God's Unfaithful Wife*, Raymond C. Ortland Jr
3 *Jesus and the Logic of History*, Paul W. Barnett
4 *Hear, My Son*, Daniel J. Estes
5 *Original Sin*, Henri Blocher
6 *Now Choose Life*, J. Gary Millar
7 *Neither Poverty nor Riches*, Craig L. Blomberg
8 *Slave of Christ*, Murray J. Harris
9 *Christ, our Righteousness*, Mark A. Seifrid
10 *Five Festal Garments*, Barry G. Webb
11 *Salvation to the Ends of the Earth*, Andreas J. Köstenberger and Peter T. O'Brien

NEW STUDIES IN BIBLICAL THEOLOGY 10

Series editor: D. A. Carson

Five festal garments

CHRISTIAN REFLECTIONS
ON
THE SONG OF SONGS
RUTH
LAMENTATIONS
ECCLESIASTES
ESTHER

Barry G. Webb

APOLLOS

INTERVARSITY PRESS
DOWNERS GROVE, ILLINOIS 60515

InterVarsity Press, USA
P.O. Box 1400
Downers Grove, IL 60515-1426, USA
World Wide Web: www.ivpress.com
Email: email@ivpress.com

APOLLOS (an imprint of Inter-Varsity Press, England)
Norton Street
Nottingham NG7 3HR, England
Website: www.ivpbooks.com
Email: ivp@ivpbooks.com

InterVarsity Press®, USA, is the book-publishing division of InterVarsity Christian Fellowship/USA® <www.intervarsity.org> and a member movement of the International Fellowship of Evangelical Students.

Inter-Varsity Press, England, is closely linked with the Universities and Colleges Christian Fellowship, a student movement connecting Christian Unions throughout Great Britain, and a member movement of the International Fellowship of Evangelical Students. Website: www.uccf.org.uk

USA ISBN 978-0-8308-2610-0
UK ISBN 978-0-85111-518-4

Typeset in Great Britain
Set in Times New Roman

Printed in the United States of America ∞

 As a member of the Green Press Initiative, InterVarsity Press is committed to protecting the environment and to the responsible use of natural resources. To learn more, visit greenpressinitiative.org.

Library of Congress Cataloging-in-Publication Data

Webb, Barry G.
  Five festal garments : Christian reflections on the Song of Songs, Ruth, Lamentations, Ecclesiastes, and Esther / Barry G. Webb.
    p. cm.— (New studies in biblical theology ; 10)
  Includes bibliographical references (p.   ) and indexes.
  ISBN 0-8308-2610-6 (pbk.: alk. paper)
  1. Bible. O.T. Five Scrolls—Criticism, interpretation, etc. I. Title II. Series: New studies in biblical theology (InterVarsity Press) ; 10.
BS1309.W43 2000
221'.044—dc21

                                                                              00-047163

British Library Cataloguing in Publication Data

A catalogue record for this book is available from the British Library.

P   23   22   21   20   19   18   17   16   15
Y   28   27   26   25   24   23   22

To George and Gladys Webb,
my first teachers in
the things of God

Contents

Series preface   9
Author's preface   11
Abbreviations   12

Introduction   13

1. The Song of Songs: Garment of love   17

2. Ruth: Garment of kindness   37

3. Lamentations: Garment of suffering   59

4. Ecclesisastes: Garment of vexation   83

5. Esther: Garment of deliverance   111

Epilogue   135

Bibliography   137
Index of modern authors   143
Index of Scripture references   145
Index of ancient sources   151

Series preface

New Studies in Biblical Theology is a series of monographs that address key issues in the discipline of biblical theology. Contributions to the series focus on one or more of three areas: 1. the nature and status of biblical theology, including its relations with other disciplines (*e.g.* historical theology, exegesis, systematic theology, historical criticism, narrative theology); 2. the articulation and exposition of the structure of thought of a particular biblical writer or corpus; and 3. the delineation of a biblical theme across all or part of the biblical corpora.

Above all, these monographs are creative attempts to help thinking Christians understand their Bibles better. The series aims simultaneously to instruct and to edify, to interact with the current literature, and to point the way ahead. In God's universe, mind and heart should not be divorced: in this series we will try not to separate what God has joined together. While the notes interact with the best of the scholarly literature, the text is uncluttered with untransliterated Greek and Hebrew, and tries to avoid too much technical jargon. The volumes are written within the framework of confessional evangelicalism, but there is always an attempt at thoughtful engagement with the sweep of the relevant literature.

This volume by Dr Barry Webb makes the Five Scrolls (the Song of Songs, Ruth, Lamentations, Ecclesiastes, Esther), the five 'Festal Garments', come alive. There is an easy grace in Dr Webb's style that masks great learning. At home with literary criticism, historical questions, the challenges of different genres, and contemporary disputes about the Scrolls, he interacts with just enough of such discussions to make his exposition rich and nuanced but not so much as to bog the reader down in endless detail. Moreover, for each scroll Dr Webb reflects on its contribution to the Old Testament, its place in Jewish liturgy, and its importance to the Christian canon. Here is biblical theology that is not reduced to atomistic reading on the one hand or to uncontrolled typology on the other. This volume will not only help thinking Christians understand their Bibles better, and therefore the God of the Bible, but (I cheerfully predict) it will form the substance of not a few sermons delivered by preachers who for the first time dare expound the Five Scrolls.

D. A. Carson
Trinity Evangelical Divinity School

Author's preface

The chapters of this book are based on the Annual Moore College Lectures delivered in Sydney, Australia, in August 1998 by invitation of the Principal, Dr Peter Jensen. I am grateful to him for giving me the opportunity to take material which I have used in lectures over many years at Moore College, and more recently at Recent College, Vancouver, to develop it further, and present it to a wider audience. My thanks are due also to the many students, colleagues and visitors who attended the lectures. Their questions and comments helped me to sharpen my thinking at many points, and encouraged me to press ahead with preparing the lectures for publication.

This project has also given me the excuse to indulge two of my greatest passions: biblical theology, and the exposition of the Old Testament as Holy Scripture which speaks powerfully to today's church. Indeed, this book is driven by the conviction that these two things are intextricably linked. It is biblical theology that enables us to see the connection between the Old Testament Scriptures and the Christian gospel and makes an authentically Christian appropriation of Old Testament books possible without doing violence to them. Each of the individual studies that comprise this book is in a sense a demonstration of this thesis. I hope they will help to stimulate a fresh appreciation of value and relevance, not just of the particular books that are studied, but of the Old Testament as a whole.

It is an honour to have this book included in New Studies in Biblical Theology. Professor D. A. Carson and Inter-Varsity Press have been extremely helpful and supportive in the difficult task of bringing the material to its present form. I dedicate this book to my parents, George and Gladys Webb. It was they who first taught me to love the Scriptures and the God who meets us there. Their prayers have been a constant source of strength to me. My father has now gone to his rest in heaven.

Barry G. Webb

Abbreviations

ANET	*Ancient Near Eastern Texts Relating to the Old Testament,* ed. J. B. Pritchard. Third edition with Supplement. Princeton: Princeton University Press, 1969.
AV	Authorized (King James) Version of the Bible (1611).
BHS	*Biblia Hebraica Stuttgartensia.*
LXX	Septuagint (ancient Greek version of the Old Testament).
MT	Masoretic Text.
NEB	New English Bible (NT 1961, second edition 1970; OT 1970).
NIV	New International Version of the Bible (1973, 1978, 1984).
NKJV	New King James Version of the Bible (1983).
NRSV	New Revised Standard Version of the Bible (1989).
NT	New Testament.
OT	Old Testament.
RSV	Revised Standard Version of the Bible (NT 1946, second edition 1971; OT 1952).
TB	Babylonian Talmud.
TJ	Jerusalem Talmud.

Introduction

The Scrolls as problem books

The works discussed in this volume are the five shortest books in the Writings, the third and final part of the Hebrew canon. Traditionally they are known simply as 'the Scrolls'.[1] I will refer to them in the following chapters as five 'garments', a metaphor that was suggested to me by the passage in Genesis 45 where Joseph is at last reconciled to his brothers. To mark the occasion he gives them all gifts, including new clothes. But to Benjamin, for whom he has a special affection, he gives 300 shekels of silver and five new outfits, or, as the RSV has it, 'five festal garments' (v. 22).

They were no doubt splendid garments, as befitted the occasion, but they must have aroused very mixed feelings in Joseph's brothers, especially the five given to Benjamin. After all, the whole sad story of conflict between them had begun with the gift of a splendid coat to one of them, a gift that had conspicuously marked him out as the favourite. There could be no question of the brothers refusing these garments, but they would always wear them rather awkwardly.

Much the same might be said of the five Scrolls. They are all problem books in one way or another, and in due course we will note the particular difficulties presented by each of them. But the basic problem has never been their canonicity. Both Israel and the church, at a relatively early stage, recognized them as gifts of divine origin that were impossible to refuse. It is virtually certain that they were included in the twenty-two books which, as Josephus in the first century AD maintained, had for generations past been accepted as Scripture by the Jewish people (*Against Apion* 1.42). If, as Roger Beckwith argues (1985: ch. 6), the standard numbers for the canonical books go back to the second century BC, the canonicity of the books in question, including that of the five Scrolls, must go back equally far. While the canonicity of some Scrolls was questioned by a minority, the real focus

[1] The *Megilloth* in Hebrew.

of the debates about these books in the first two centuries AD lay elsewhere, namely, the congruence of the Scrolls with other canonical books, and the manner in which they should be understood and used as Holy Scripture. In other words, the key issue was how the Scrolls were to be 'worn'. The solution that eventually emerged in Judaism was their adoption as lectionary readings for five of the major festivals: Passover (Song of Songs), the Feast of Weeks (Ruth), the Ninth of Ab (Lamentations), the Feast of Tabernacles (Ecclesiastes) and the Festival of Purim (Esther).

No comparable solution has emerged in Christianity, however. There seems no reason to doubt that all five Scrolls were accepted as Scripture in most parts of the church from the first century. But no consensus has emerged about their proper use, or about how they address us as Christians. They are among the most neglected books of the Christian Bible. Each of them in its own way poses for us in an acute form the question how the Old Testament can be the word of God for us today. This question will be the main focus of the following chapters, with the five Scrolls as case studies.

'Christian reflections': a biblical-theological approach

I have subtitled these studies 'Christian reflections'. They are Christian first of all in the sense that I myself am a Christian and will make no attempt to disguise this. They are also Christian in the more intentional sense that the ultimate goal of each study is to identify how the book in question relates to the Christian gospel as presented in the New Testament by Jesus Christ and his apostles. This is where biblical theology plays an absolutely crucial role.

Biblical theology is something of an ugly duckling in biblical studies. It has 'turned up', so to speak, in the world of academia and seems to think that it belongs there. But the other members of the brood have been thrown into a degree of alarm and consternation by its presence, for they are not at all sure that it is really one of them. It appears to be a somewhat odd mixture of dogmatic theology (which is for 'true believers') and historical and literary study of the Bible (which is for serious critical scholars).[2] Most find it easier to say what it is not than

---

[2] The beginnings of biblical theology as a discipline are normally traced to Gabler's 1787 lecture on the distinction between biblical and dogmatic theology. But the kind of biblical theology with which we are concerned here is quite different from Gabler's, and has flourished in the last couple of decades at the same time as (and partly under the

to say what it is. Biblical theology is not doctrinal theology, history of religion, biblical criticism, study of the biblical languages or natural theology. In his recent major work on biblical theology, James Barr begins by defining it in precisely this negative way. 'Biblical theology is essentially a *contrastive notion*', and its multifaceted character is most clearly seen when we are clear about how it differs from other recognized forms of biblical and theological study (1999: 5). But as Barr himself rightly recognizes, neither is it *wholly* distinct from any of them. The most difficult questions of all arise, however, when one tries to move into positive mode and define exactly what biblical theology *is*.

This is not the place to embark on a survey of all the ways in which biblical theology as an academic discipline has been defined and practised from Johann Philipp Gabler in the late eighteenth century to the present time. That would require another work, much larger than this one, and in any case would duplicate what has already been done very adequately by others.[3] What is necessary here is for me to make clear the kind of biblical theology to which I am personally committed and will practise in the following chapters. Its origins and distinctives have recently been discussed in three articles by Donald Robinson, Graeme Goldsworthy and myself that were originally presented at a conference at Moore College in 1996, and have now been published with other, related, papers, in *Interpreting God's Plan: Biblical Theology and the Pastor* (Gibson 1997). It is an approach that sees the fundamental task of the discipline as describing as fully as possible the given, canonical shape of the Bible's own theology. Its focus is on the unity of Scripture, *while doing full justice to its diversity*. The key to this unity in diversity is found in the gospel preached by Jesus and his apostles, to which the New Testament bears witness. This gospel is everywhere anchored in the Old Testament, of which it is seen to be the fulfilment. In short, the kind of biblical theology that will be practised here is an evangelical one, not just in the sense that (some) evangelicals practise it, but in that it derives its rationale from the evangel (the gospel) itself.

For Christians, the word of God is essentially Jesus Christ, and the gospel that announces what God has accomplished in him. Therefore

---

influence of) significant new developments in hermeneutics. In a forthcoming article, Vanhoozer speaks of 'the second coming of biblical theology in the twentieth century' (Vanhoozer, 'Exegesis and hermeneutics').

[3] For a concise but helpful treatment, with references to the relevant literature, see Carson 1995.

the question of how any part of the Bible is the word of God for us necessarily and centrally involves the issue of how it relates to the gospel. At the same time, respect for the biblical text as Scripture requires that each book be allowed to be what it is, and not be forced to speak with a voice that is not its own. Part of the richness of the biblical gospel is the diversity of testimony to it, both directly in the New Testament and indirectly in the Old.

With this in mind I will adopt the following approach. The first step for each book will be to undertake a reading of it in which the aim will be to let the book set its own agenda, unconstrained by questions beyond the horizon of whoever gave it its final shape. This will involve reference to other parts of the Old Testament, but only in so far as we are led out into this wider context by the text itself. The second step will be to explore the relationship of the book to its Old Testament context in a more systematic way. The final step will be to grapple with how the book relates to the New Testament gospel with its basic 'promise and fulfilment' structure. Each chapter is divided into three sections (marked I, II, III) corresponding to these three steps.

I have used the term 'reflections' in the subtitle to acknowledge the subjective element that is necessarily part of any act of interpretation. What are presented here are readings, subject to correction by other readings that share the same basic hermeneutical commitments. The term 'reflections' is also intended to temper the expectations of the audience. Obviously, exhaustive exegesis is impossible within the limits of space available in this volume. As far as possible I will allow the books themselves, by the way they are structured, and the agenda they set in passages which are thus thrown into prominence, to alert us to the major issues that need to be pursued within the framework of the general approach I have outlined.[4]

---

[4] For a full treatment of the issues involved in the method I have outlined here see Webb 1997.

Chapter One

The Song of Songs
Garment of love

In my youth they used to make me read the Bible.
Trouble was, the only books I took to naturally were
the ones they weren't over and above keen on. But I
got to know the Song of Songs pretty well
by heart.
Lord Peter Wimsey[1]

Two problems confront any reader of the Song of Songs. The first is
the problem of meaning. Who is speaking to whom, and what do they
mean when they say what they say? The second has to do with the
place of the book in the canon of Scripture. How are we to read it as
part of the Bible? How does it relate to the message of the Bible as a
whole? Of course, these problems are not unique to the Song of Songs.
We have to grapple with them when we read any biblical book. But
they present themselves in an especially acute form when we come to
this particular book.

I

The Song as love poetry

The starting-point must be to recognize that what lies before us on the
page is love poetry. It is rich in imagery, much of it very sensuous.
Take, for example, the opening lines of the poem (1:2):

---

[1] In Dorothy L. Sayers' short story, *The Vindictive Story of the Footsteps that Ran*
(cited in Carr 1993: 281). Carr comments: 'Whether the Dowager Duchess was wise or
not in monitoring her son's literary career is beside the point – at least she had a clear
understanding of what the Song is all about.'

> Let him kiss me with the kisses of his mouth –
> for your love is better than wine ... [2]

'Let him kiss me' is sensuous in itself, but here that particular quality of the language is intensified by the additional words, 'with the kisses of his mouth'. And this is just the beginning. In what follows there is going to be a lot of description of the various parts of the male and female body and of the delights of seeing, touching, tasting, hearing and smelling. As for imagery, love-making is compared here to the drinking of wine, with its strong connotations of intoxication and physical pleasure, and again it is but a beginning; more extravagant imagery will follow as the Song unfolds. The Song, as the name suggests, has a strong lyrical quality. The lines are short and rhythmical, and deal more with feelings than with rationally presented objective truth, and this requires a special kind of sensitivity from us. When the woman says that the love of her man is 'better than wine', it would of course be absurd for us to want to know whether it *really is* better than wine in any way that could be empirically or rationally established. It is simply not that kind of statement. The words are a true expression of how this woman *feels* about his love, and that is all that matters. We will need to maintain this kind of sensitivity, even when the need for it may be less obvious. The Song is love poetry from beginning to end.

Its subject is love, but it is neither a philosophical treatise about love, nor a sex manual. It is a rhapsody of love, an outpouring of the feelings of people who are in love and are experiencing it in the flesh, with all its attendant pains and pleasures. There is an intimacy about the book which is both delightful and embarrassing. The lovers are not aware of our presence. What they say, they say to each other and not to us. What they do, they do to each other and not to us. In a sense, the book is not addressed to us at all – and yet it is, for by simply *being there* for us to read it opens a window for us into that intimate world and allows us to experience in some measure what the lovers themselves are experiencing. This is a book for those who want to know, or perhaps remember, what it is like to be in love and to make love.

But how are we to understand the voices that we hear in the Song?

---

[2] My translation. The more interpretive NIV rendering is 'more delightful than wine'. The shift from the third person ('Let him kiss me') to the second person ('your love') has given rise to various emendations, but none of them has hard textual support, and such shifts in person are common in love poetry; cf. Deut. 32:15; Is. 1:29; Jer. 22:24; Mic. 1:19; Ps. 23. See Pope 1977: 297.

Are they the voices of a particular pair of lovers whose relationship may be traced throughout the book? Is there just one pair of lovers, or several? Or is the whole quest to identify particular lovers misguided? Should we rather take the voices simply as that – voices, male and female respectively, speaking out typical expressions of love, as in modern love lyrics?[3]

At least one lover, Solomon, is named in the Song, and there is a description of his wedding in 3:6–11.[4] We may perhaps be forgiven for wondering which one, since Solomon seems not to have known where to draw the line when it came to weddings! But no such considerations seem to trouble the writer. Only one wedding is mentioned, and it is a splendid and happy occasion. Two other lovers appear to be more or less clearly identified, although they are not named. The first is a rather naïve country girl, called the 'Shulammite' in 6:13. This is probably a place name (maid of Shulam), but the location is so far unknown. The second is a male shepherd lover who is so idealized that he scarcely seems to touch the ground: 'he pastures his flocks among the lilies' (6:3, my translation). And beside these two there is a host of minor figures: mother, brothers, watchmen, women of Jerusalem and others.

So there appears to be a considerable cast of characters, and this has led most commentators to assume that the Song is a drama of some kind. But the variations on this basic approach have been many. It has been seen as involving two main characters: Solomon and the Shulammite; or three: Solomon and the two country lovers (Solomon is an intruder). Some have seen it as a cultic drama, the expurgated liturgy of a fertility cult. And among those who have seen it as a drama there has been disagreement about whether it should be interpreted allegorically or literally (see Falk 1982: 62–63). The basic problem with reading the book as a drama is that the plot is very difficult to follow, and this stems mainly from uncertainty about Solomon's role. In spite of attempts to do so, he cannot simply be equated with the shepherd figure, since in the Song there is an explicit distancing of Solomon's world from the world of the lovers (8:11). But neither can he easily be regarded as an intruder in their world, for this would cast him in the role of a villain, and he can hardly be that in a book which is either by him or for him (1:1),[5] and in which he is, if anything, idealized rather than vilified (1:5; 3:11).

---

[3] The contrast I have in mind is with old-style love ballads which have a narrative thread and distinct characters.

[4] He is also named at 1:1, 5; 8:11–12.

[5] The Hebrew expression *lišlōmōh* can mean either 'by' or 'for' Solomon. Cf. the

An anthology of love lyrics?

The apparently insoluble nature of these problems has been a major factor in the current trend, which has become almost universal in recent interpretations of the Song, to read it as a *collection* of love lyrics rather than as a single poem. Its unity is sought through a study of recurring themes, settings and motifs rather than through plot and character. The country girl, the shepherd and the king (see 1:4, 12; 7:5) are all taken to be conventional figures rather than characters in the normal sense.[6] Solomon himself is seen not as a participant in the love-making of the poem, but as an ideal figure whose name is invoked from time to time because of the rich connotations it has. He is a patron and symbol rather than a suitor. Sometimes unity of a different kind is found in the presence of chiasms and other formal structures. But essentially what unifies the poems, on this view, is that they are all exemplars of the same kind of love poetry. Any semblance of plot or of a developing relationship between particular lovers is illusory and should be disregarded.

Marcia Falk's *Love Lyrics from the Bible* (1982) is a sensitive study of the book in this mode. Her division of the work into thirty-one poems is based on literary and structural analysis, with particular attention to changes of setting, subject matter, speaker, audience, mood and so on. She admits that this is highly subjective and that others differ from her in the number of poems they recognize; but she maintains that this does not greatly matter. What her analysis focuses on ultimately are themes which transcend the individual poems. She finds three voices in the poems: singular male, singular female and the voice of a group of onlookers. That is all they are, however – voices. The poems are not about particular lovers, but about love itself.

She identifies four 'contexts' or settings which recur throughout the collection. There are two basic settings, country and city, and each of these has two further sub-categories. For convenience, we may be display them as follows (the diagram is my own, not Falk's):

---

heading to Ps. 18, where similar expressions are used to indicate both authorship by David and assignment of the psalm to the choirmaster.

[6] Cf. the beautiful woman and the swooning lover in the Petrarchan sonnet tradition of Italian and English love poetry.

THE SONG OF SONGS: GARMENT OF LOVE

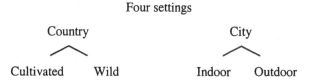

Four settings

Country   City

Cultivated   Wild   Indoor   Outdoor

A different mood is created by each setting. The cultivated countryside consists of pastures where shepherds graze their flocks, and of woodlands, gardens, vineyards and gentle valleys full of flowers. These are symbols of paradise, and in this setting love is innocent and ideal, like that of Adam and Eve before the fall (1:15–17). An entirely different mood is created by reference to scorching sun, storm, lightning and flood (8:6–7). Here love is linked with the powerful, elemental forces of nature. Love is not all sweetness; it can also be a torrential force, destroying all in its path. Within the city, indoor settings – the king's chambers, the speaker's bedroom, the mother's house – are supportive environments for love. Here love can take its course away from prying eyes (3:1–4). In contrast, the city streets constitute a hostile environment where disdain, disapproval and even physical violence are encountered (5:7–9). Against these backgrounds, love is presented in its many aspects: love innocent and ideal, love torrential and powerful, love privately enjoyed, love threatened – the many faces of love.

In addition, five recurring themes are identified. The first is what Falk calls 'the beckoning of the beloved'. The invitation to love takes many forms: elaborate praise of the beloved (4:1–7), entreaty ('Arise, my love ... and come away', 2:10, my translation), or description of the lush countryside (the implicit argument is, 'All nature is mating, why not we?', cf. 2:11–13).[7] In tension with this is the second theme, 'the banishment of the beloved'. Courtship is interrupted because of the disapproval of family members, and the voluntary but painful separation of the lovers (she tells him to leave). This produces moments of great pathos (2:17; 4:6; 8:14). The third theme, 'the search for the beloved', deals with the sense of loss that is experienced whenever the beloved is not near (3:1–5; 5:2 – 6:3). The fourth theme, 'the self in a hostile world', is about the sense of self-worth that comes from loving and being loved (1:5), and the final theme, 'the praise of love itself', simply makes explicit what is implied in the other four (8:6–7). Collectively, these themes indicate that

[7] Cf. such classics in the English tradition as Andrew Marvell's *To His Coy Mistress*.

... the emotional fabric of the Song is not wholly joyful, but sometimes interwoven with tensions and struggle ... Taken as a whole, the Song expresses the paradoxes of love in the world: conflict which intensifies passion, painful separation which heightens the pleasure of union, bonding which gives the individual courage to stand alone (Falk 1982: 96–97).[8]

Clearly, there is a great deal that is valuable in such a study. It helps us to appreciate the richly lyrical character of the Song, its finely modulated emotional and tonal quality, and the many facets of love that it presents. But for all that, I believe that the division of the text into separate poems is unnecessary and unhelpful. There is strong evidence that the Song is in fact a single love poem, and much is lost if we fail to read it as such.

Indications of unity

The title

The expression 'Song of Songs' (1:1) has the same form in Hebrew as the the better-known 'Holy of Holies'.[9] It does not mean 'the song consisting of many songs', but 'the song to end all songs', 'the greatest song'. The title tells us that what lies before us is a single song. Therefore, if we wish to read the Song as Holy Scripture – as part of the canon – we must first discipline our minds to read it as a single poem, for the title itself is part of the canonical form of the Song. When we do so we shall find plenty of evidence of unity within the body of the Song itself.

The refrain

A refrain occurs in almost identical form at three points in the Song (2:7; 3:5; 8:4). It is addressed to the women of Jerusalem:

Daughters of Jerusalem, I charge you

---

[8] Falk goes on to explore in more detail the 'lighter strands' of the Song's meaning through a study of six central motifs: flora and fauna, vines and vineyard, the garden, eating and drinking, regality and wealth, sensuality and the senses. Carr (1981: 98) notes that 'every generation of every society has its love-song tradition', and that the most common theme is the joy and excitement the lovers find in each other's presence. 'Of course separation, caused by some outside person or situation, is frequently encountered, but even these experiences serve primarily as a foil to underscore the joy of reunion.'

[9] Cf. the NT expressions, 'King of kings', 'Lord of lords', Rev. 17:14; 19:16.

> by the gazelles and by the does of the field:
> Do not arouse or awaken love
> until it so desires.[10]

The gist of this is, 'Don't interfere. Let love take its natural course. The consummation will come at its proper time' (cf. Carr 1984: 94). This refrain creates anticipation and suspense. It suggests a relationship between two people moving steadily towards consummation in spite of separation, hostility and interference from others. It encourages us to look for progression towards a climax.

The climax

The way the Song ends shows clearly that the anticipated consummation has been reached (8:5–7). The lovers walk together openly arm in arm, perfectly at ease at last in each other's company and fearing no-one's censure (8:5; contrast v. 2). As they approach the girl's parental home, they reminisce happily about the past: 'Under the apple tree I awakened [NIV "roused"] you' (that is where they fell in love), and 'there [probably in the house] your mother conceived you' (that is where the girl was born). Anxious anticipation has given way to happy reminiscence; they are man and wife at last. There is no torrid sex scene at this point, for the true consummation of love is not sex, but relationship – the sort of relationship portrayed here. As they walk, she leans upon her beloved (8:5a). It is a little cameo of the married relationship as envisaged in both the Old and the New Testament.

The woman's appeal to the man to confirm his undying commitment to her (8:6a) becomes the occasion for a whole series of reflections on the nature of love: it is as strong as death, as hard as Sheol, a blazing flame, unquenchable and priceless (8:6b–7). In 'death', 'Sheol' (NIV mg.) and 'flame' there is the hint of dark and destructive possibilities, and hence the women's need for reassurance that her beloved will be faithful. But at the same time there is an implied affirmation of the indestructible power of love; it is equal to all challenges, even those of death and Sheol.[11] And the closing note is unquestionably positive; all the wealth of a man's house is contemptible compared to the value of love. It is beyond price.

Reflection on this passage is critical for a proper appreciation of how

---

[10] The only variation is that the second line is omitted in 8:4.

[11] Cf. Landy (1979: 523): 'Only Love is as strong as Death, and is therefore of supreme value; Death destroys all but love … (8:7).' As Landy notes, Pope (1977: 210–219) argues that the Song of Songs emanates from a funeral feast.

the book works. The movement to generalizations about the nature of love itself, as distinct from the particulars of his love for her and *vice versa*, is a strong indication that a point of consummation has been reached. It confirms that the cameo of the couple presented in 8:5 is indeed the climax of the Song. It is time for reflection on, and drawing conclusions from, all that has been presented. And it is here that the author comes closer to addressing us directly than at any point since the title in 1:1. The conjunction 'for' in 8:6b, 'for love is as strong as death ...', binds the woman's appeal in 8:6a to what follows and makes the whole speech from there on hers. But the nature of the speech is different from any of her previous ones. It is natural, therefore, to assume that at this point she has become the author's mouthpiece, and speaks for him[12] as well as for herself. This, combined with the fact that the language is akin to the wisdom language of Proverbs, and that the title has explicitly linked the book with Solomon, strongly suggests that the Song is intended to have a didactic dimension to it. It is meant to lead us, via its presentation of the love of this man and this woman, to reflection on the nature of love itself.

Finally, it can hardly be without significance that it is at this point that we have the only, if veiled, reference in the book to God. Love is the 'flame of Yah' (*šalheḇetyāh*). It could be that the abbreviated divine name Yah (= Yahweh) on the end of this word is used simply to indicate a superlative, and it is so taken by the NIV, 'a mighty flame'. But the context speaks against this. 'Yah' is used here in close conjunction with 'jealousy' (*qin'â*) and 'fire' (*'ēš*), both of which are closely associated with Yahweh in Israelite tradition.[13] Furthermore, it is most fitting that there should be an allusion to Yahweh when the poem moves transparently into wisdom mode, since the very first principle of Old Testament wisdom is the fear of Yahweh. More particularly, what is being suggested is that the love depicted here, and hence in the Song as a whole, has its ultimate source in Yahweh, and indeed partakes of his very nature. In keeping with the allusive character of the Song, however, this powerful point is made with exquisite indirectness rather than being forced crudely upon us. The Song is not as secular as at first it appears.

---

[12] Or for her. I use 'him' without prejudice as to the sex of the author.

[13] Cf. Landy (1979: 524 n. 40): 'The divine reference here is extremely controverted. Nevertheless, in the context of the declaration that Love is as as strong as Death, as powerful as Sheol, the possibility that it is "the flame of Yahweh" is very suggestive ... Indeed the metaphor of fire frequently signifies God in the Old Testament (e.g. Deut. 4:24 or the burning bush).'

The coda

As in many musical compositions, after the climax comes a concluding movement (8:8–14), which quietly echoes some of the major themes of the work and brings it to a close. We have space here for comment on verse 10 only:

> I am a wall
> and my breasts are like towers;
> Thus I have become in his eyes
> as one who brings peace.[14]

In view of the immediately preceding context (8:8–9), this image of the woman as a wall with breasts like towers in verse 10 clearly refers simultaneously to her sexual maturity and to her chastity. She kept herself for her lover, and for this reason was one who brought him peace (*šālôm*), complete sexual fulfilment. The significant word *šālôm* is a backward, summary comment on the consummation portrayed in 8:5, and brings to completion the movement of the entire Song from ardent longing to satisfied rest.[15]

The dream sequence

Between the expressions of longing at the beginning and the consummation that is reached at the end, there is a dream sequence. Its precise limits are difficult to define (my own view is that it spans chs. 3 – 6), but it certainly exists. Take, for example, 3:1:

> All night long on my bed
> I looked for the one my heart loves …

or even more clearly, 5:2:

> I slept but my heart was awake.

In this central part of the Song the bride-to-be is dreaming about her wedding day and the love-making that will follow. In these chapters we find everything we might expect in such circumstances: erotic fantasies, nightmares, fears of losing her lover, and romantic transformations of him into a prince and of her own wedding day into a grand, royal

---

[14] The NIV has 'like one bringing contentment'.

[15] Cf. the similar use of *šālôm* in the final chapter of the book of Esther (Est. 10:3).

occasion. In fact it is not Solomon's wedding she dreams about in 3:6–11, but her own (cf. Fleming 1982: 95). Confirmation, if needed, is provided by 6:12 (RSV):

> Before I was aware, my fancy set me
> in a chariot beside my prince.[16]

and more significantly, by the repetition of 3:6 ('Who is this coming up from the desert?') in 8:5, where fantasy at last gives way to reality.[17] Solomon is not an intruder into the relationship between the lovers, but a somewhat remote, ideal figure, who merges with the shepherd in the girl's dreams.

Rightly understood, then, the Song is a single poem about a love relationship between two people, in which fantasy and reality, idealism and realism, are held together in a delicate balance.

The realism and idealism of the Song

There is profound realism in the Song. The author knows how hard it is to wait. He knows about erotic dreams. He knows about meddling relatives and busybodies (the brothers and the women of Jerusalem). He knows about the struggle to establish a relationship in the face of interference and hostility. He knows that love can get out of control and become cruel and destructive (8:6). The girl dreams of love, but she also dreams of rape (5:7):

> The watchmen found me
> as they made their rounds in the city.
> they beat me, they bruised me;
> they took away my cloak,
> those watchmen of the walls!

She longs for love, but she also fears it, and as she dreams her fears rise up and confront her. The author knows that we do not live any more in the Garden of Eden, but in a fallen world where love can easily turn into lust and where love-making can become rape.

---

[16] 'My fancy' here (literally 'my soul') corresponds to 'my heart' in 5:2. The girl is still dreaming.

[17] Fantasy also gives way to reality in another sense. In the body of the Song the girl has dreamed about bringing her lover home to her mother's house (3:4); at the climax of the Song she actually does so (8:5).

But there is also idealism here, and in fact this is the dominant note. The overwhelming impression that the Song leaves us with is that love is a beautiful thing, almost too beautiful for words to express. It shows us love as a profoundly fulfilling thing in which we may find deep contentment and satisfaction. It shows us a world in which a shepherd may become a prince in the eyes of his beloved, a world in which wealth and power are irrelevant. This Song puts wealth and power in their place. Take, for example, 8:11–12 (RSV) where, as we have seen, the Song is winding down to its quiet conclusion:

> [11] Solomon had a vineyard at Baal-hamon;
>   he let out the vineyard to keepers ...
> [12] My vineyard, my very own, is for myself;
>   you, O Solomon, may have the thousand,
>   and the keepers of the fruit two hundred.

The 'vineyard' of verse 12 is the girl's body with its capacity for sexual pleasure (cf. 1:6). Solomon's 'vineyard' in verse 11 is his harem.[18] Paradoxically, the more women Solomon has, the less deeply personal and fulfilling can be his relationship with any one of them. He has to hire 'keepers'. The shepherd does not begrudge him his wealth, nor does he envy him. Solomon has *his* vineyard and the shepherd has his own, his *very own*, and with her he is well content.[19] The Song shows us a world in which a shepherd and a country girl can be as happy and fulfilled as the king upon his throne – perhaps even more so.

We turn now from the Song itself to a consideration of it as part of the Hebrew Bible.

II

The chief difficulty that certain rabbis of the first and second centuries AD felt with the Song was its secularity; that it apparently dealt with merely human matters rather than divine. The answer was found in mystical interpretation of it, whereby its real theme was found to be the love of Yahweh for Israel. The rabbis did not absolutely repudiate the literal interpretation, for they were not prudish about married love, but did strongly object to the book being quoted or sung lasciviously, and

---

[18] Cf. Solomon's thousand here with 700 wives and 300 concubines in 1 Kgs. 11:3.

[19] The speaker in 8:12 may be the girl rather than the shepherd, but the general import is the same.

emphasized its mystical meaning. This kind of understanding of the Song is already implicit in Rabbi Akiva's famous first-century defence of it as the Holy of Holies:

> No man in Israel ever disputed, concerning the Song of Songs, that it did not make the hands unclean, for the whole world is not worth the day on which the Song of Songs was given to Israel; for all the Hagiographa are holy, but the Song of Songs is the Holy of Holies (Mishnah *Yadaim* 3.5).[20]

The mystical interpretation reached its full development in mainstream Judaism in the Targum to the Song of Songs, probably from the seventh century AD, in which five movements are identified in it, corresponding to five periods in Yahweh's covenant relationship with Israel, from the exodus and giving of the law to the Roman diaspora and the coming of the Messiah.[21] All this eventually found liturgical expression in the reading of the Song of Songs at the Passover, Judaism's celebration *par excellence* of God's saving love for his people (cf. Peterson 1992: 27–33).

It would be foolhardy indeed to dismiss such a venerable tradition out of hand. It draws a certain plausibility from Isaiah 5:1–7, 'I will sing for the one I love a song about his vineyard ...', and from the way the Old Testament prophets depict the relationship between Yahweh and Israel as a covenanted love relationship.[22] According to Jeremiah in particular, the wilderness period, when Israel was given the law and the Passover was instituted, was the honeymoon period of this love (Jer. 2:1–3).[23] The adoption of the Song of Songs as a lectionary reading for Passover has recently been described as a stroke of pastoral genius

[20] In rabbinic terms, to say that a book 'made the hands unclean' was to say that it was divinely inspired. Why contact with holy books was held to make the hands unclean is unclear. For a full discussion see Beckwith 1985: 278–283. Beckwith's own view, based on indirect evidence from rabbinic sources, is as follows: 'By declaring that the Scriptures made the hands unclean, the rabbis protected them from careless and irreverent treatment, since it is obvious that no one would be so apt to handle them heedlessly if he were every time obliged to wash his hands afterwards.'

[21] The allegorical referents of the major divisions are as follows: (1) The exodus and entry into Canaan (1:2 – 3:6); (2) Solomon's temple (3:7 – 5:1); (3) Sin and exile (5:2 – 6:1); (4) Rebuilding the temple (6:2 – 7:11); (5) The Roman diaspora and the coming of the Messiah (7:12 – 8:14). Cf. Loewe 1966: 170–173.

[22] Cf. Landy (1979: 28): 'That love songs were capable of being allegorised is clear from Isaiah's parable [Is. 5:1–7]'.

[23] Cf. Hos. 2:14, where to lead Israel back into the wilderness and speak tenderly to her is to woo her back to her first, pure love for Yahweh. Here, as often, there is a very close connection between Jeremiah and Hosea.

which saved redemption from ever being reduced to a mere dogma or ritual (Peterson 1992: 29–30). To be redeemed is to be loved, and to be called to love in return, and the Song of Songs as part of the Passover liturgy is a powerful annual reminder of this fact. It is the way Israel found to read the Song as Holy Scripture, and it is to this that we probably owe its preservation. It has also had a powerful influence on the way in which Christians have traditionally read the Song.[24] Nevertheless, the allegorization on which it depends is open to serious question and must, in the final analysis, be rejected if the Song is to be allowed to be what it is and to speak with its own voice.

The Song as wisdom literature

The explicit connection with the rest of the Old Testament which the text of the Song itself provides is its title, which associates it with Solomon and therefore with the wisdom literature. This of itself does not rule out taking it as an allegory, since allegory is an attested form of Old Testament wisdom discourse. However, there is nothing in the Song itself that indicates it is such, and the title militates strongly against reading into it themes that are not at all typical of the wisdom literature. In marked contrast to the prophetic books, this literature characteristically deals not with the great saving events of Israel's history, but with the everyday world of human relationships. We are therefore on much surer ground if we do not read the Song as an allegory of Yahweh's relationship with Israel, but rather relate it conceptually to a wisdom passage such as Proverbs 5:15–19:

> Drink water from your own cistern,
> running water from your own well ...
> [17] Let them be yours alone,
> never to be shared with strangers.
> [18] May your fountain be blessed,
> and may you rejoice in the wife of your youth.
> [19] A loving doe, a graceful deer –
> may her breasts satisfy you always,
> may you ever be captivated by her love.

The verbal links with the Song of Songs are striking; the words

---

[24] For a reasonably complete review of the history of Christian interpretation up to and including the nineteenth century see Pope 1977: 112–132.

translated 'drink', 'water', 'well', 'breasts' and 'love' are all shared, and used in basically the same way. And the 'loving doe' and 'graceful deer' of this passage cannot help but call to mind the 'gazelles' and 'does' of the Song. Both deal with the delight of sexual intimacy which properly belongs within a covenanted relationship between a man and a woman. What is explicit in Proverbs is implicit in the Song, and what is enjoined by way of instruction in Proverbs is celebrated as an experienced reality in the Song. But the basic subject matter is the same, and it is noteworthy that Solomon, with whom both works are associated, is traditionally credited with composing both proverbs and songs (1 Kgs. 4:32). Furthermore, we have observed how the Song moves into a typically didactic, wisdom style of discourse at its climax (8:6–7).

The Song and Genesis 1 – 3

While it is less explicitly signalled, the Song also has a close affinity with the 'creation and fall' narrative of Genesis 1 – 3. There are a number of ways in which this connection is suggested: by the tension between idealism and realism in the Song, by the centrality of the garden motif (4:8 – 5:1), and especially by the way the Song as a whole resonates with the climax reached at the end of Genesis 2. There, after the creation of the woman and the man's joyful acknowledgment of her as his partner, the author comments: 'The man and his wife were both naked, and they felt no shame' (v. 25).

This statement is both a recognition of the goodness of what has been given, and a bridge to the tragic loss of it which follows. With some justification the Song of Songs may be seen as a kind of extended commentary or poetic meditation on this verse.[25] But the precise nature of that meditation will become apparent only as we attend carefully to the details of the text.

I have already drawn attention to the presence of negative elements in the Song, but these are in fact more numerous than first meets the eye. There is the harshness and possessiveness of the brothers (1:6; 8:8–9), the little foxes that ruin the vineyards (2:15), the sexual violence of the watchmen (5:7), and the brooding presence of death and the grave (8:6). The woman is certainly abused by men. Whatever their motives, the brothers appear to regard her as their property, and the watchmen's

---

[25] See Barth 1960: 292–300, and cf. Lys 1968: 52: 'Le Cantique n'est rien d'autre qu'un commentaire de Gen. 2' ('The Song is nothing other than a commentary on Gen. 2').

disregard for her dignity is crude and explicit. But she also suffers abuse of a more subtle kind at the hands of other women, whose disdainful looks and questions force her, more than once, to defend both herself and her beloved (1:6; 5:9–16). In terms of Genesis 3, these signs of disorder in the world of nature and human relationships are manifestations of the fall. And against this background, the love experienced by the lovers becomes a kind of return to Eden (cf. Landy 1979). To love as they do is to enter a garden and to be satiated with its abundant fruit and fragrant perfumes (4:12 – 5:1). It is to taste again the unalloyed goodness of the gift once given.

It is not, however, as some feminist readings of the Song have maintained (e.g. Trible 1973; 1978), to return to a state of total, unqualified equality between man and woman, as though this were the created ideal.[26] It is true that there is a striking egalitarianism in the way the lovers conduct their sexual relationship. The Song begins and ends with the woman speaking, and she is very active throughout their love-making, sharing the initiative fully with the man. Her longings for him are fully answered by his desire for her (7:10). They express their need for each other without constraint, and without either reducing the other to mere compliance. They are fully partners in the giving and receiving of love. Yet it would be wrong to describe their relationship as unstructured, or purely symmetrical. At the beginning of the Song she sits in his shade (2:3), and at the climax, where the nature of their relationship is crystallized, she leans upon him (8:5). In other words, it is he who provides the secure environment in which she can be free to express her sexual needs without constraint. And paradoxically, if we read the Song correctly, one of the most important ways he does this is by being totally open about his own need for her. They need each other, and the drive towards the 'one flesh' relationship of sexual intimacy is a drive towards *šālôm* ('peace, wholeness'; 8:10).

Contribution to Old Testament theology

What then can we say about the Song in its Old Testament context? Here we move beyond the motivation of those who first placed it there, or defended it, to consider how it actually functions in that context when it is allowed make its own unique contribution. Many things could be said, but we confine ourselves to three.

It affirms the essential goodness of bodily existence and sexual

---

[26] For a perceptive critique of Trible see Charry 1987: 203–209.

relationships against those who may be tempted to denigrate them in the interests of a 'pure', higher form of religion. In the words of the distinguished Jewish scholar, Robert Gordis,

> Over and beyond its eternal youthfulness and inherent charm, the Song of Songs, precisely because it is within the canon of Scripture, serves to broaden the horizons of religion. It gives expression, in poetic and hence deathless terms, to the authentic world-view of Judaism, which denies any dichotomy between body and soul, between matter and spirit, because it recognises them both as twin aspects of the great and unending miracle called life (1974: 44).

Love – this kind of love – is the very flame of Yahweh.

Equally, and as a corollary of this, it resists any tendency to idealize singleness as, in itself, a superior state. To rejoice in the wife of one's youth, to be satisfied by her breasts and captivated by her love is to walk in the path of the wisdom that is grounded in the fear of Yahweh. The drive towards one-flesh union with one's bride or groom is a drive towards wholeness. The Song affirms powerfully, in its own way, the truth of the divine pronouncement that it is 'not good' for a man to be alone (Gen. 2:18); nor is it good for a woman. It follows that those who remain single, for whatever reason, suffer real deprivation. There is no romanticism about singleness in the Old Testament.

Finally, by the way it depicts the consummation of the relationship between the lovers, and by celebrating sexual love without reference to procreation, the Song implicitly teaches that the bonding of man and woman into a one-flesh unity is the primary function of sex. I have argued elsewhere (Webb 1994) that this is also implicit in Genesis 1 – 2, and commented on its significant ethical implications. We simply note here that, once again, the Song underlines an important aspect of the teaching of those chapters, which in many ways are foundational for the theology of the Old Testament as a whole.

III

What the Song of Songs says as part of the Old Testament it also says as part of the Christian Bible, but in this larger context it is brought into connection with the gospel and with the teaching of the New Testament in general.

The Song and the New Testament teaching about sex and marriage

There is no conflict here with the distinctives of the Song. The New Testament, like the Song of Songs, recognizes the negative effects of the fall, but affirms the essential goodness of life in the body[27] and of sex within marriage,[28] and the primacy of the unitive aspect of sex (Webb 1994: 99–101). It is striking in this regard that when Jesus Christ speaks explicitly about the God-ordained nature of marriage, it is specifically the 'one-flesh' passage, Genesis 2:25, that he quotes.[29]

The one area in which a tension suggests itself is in the matter of singleness, especially singleness for the sake of the kingdom of heaven (Matt. 19:12), as exemplified by Jesus himself. But, properly understood, this is simply a recognition that dedication to God involves self-sacrifice, and is part of a broader teaching about the nature of discipleship. The true disciple must be willing to forgo marriage, home, loved ones, even life itself if need be, for the sake of the kingdom.[30] This is no more an idealization of singleness than of homelessness or death. In fact, it is a strong affirmation of the goodness of marriage, and a recognition of the very real deprivation involved in singleness.[31]

---

[27] As in the NT teaching about the resurrection of the body, and particularly the bodily resurrection of Christ, e.g. 1 Cor. 15, esp. vv. 35–49.

[28] Heb. 13:4.

[29] Matt. 19:5–6; Mark 10:8. Cf. the apostle Paul in 1 Cor. 6:16; Eph. 5:31.

[30] Matt. 8:20; Luke 9:24, 58; 14:33.

[31] Complex and sensitive issues arise here. Clearly, singleness is not to be seen as inferior to marriage in all respects, and single persons should not be viewed as 'incomplete' in any way that calls into question their integrity and dignity as human beings. Nevertheless, the Song of Songs has something important to say in this area, and it must be allowed to make its contribution to a fully biblical approach to these matters. I have argued in this chapter that the Song must be read against the background of Gen. 1 – 3. There, the statement 'It is not good for the man to be alone' (2:18) stands in stark contrast to the long string of pronouncements in Gen. 1, 'It was good ... good ... very good'. Here at last is something (aloneness) that is *not* good. The *good* condition that answers to this is the 'one flesh' union between the man and the woman that is reached in Gen. 2:23–25. The whole Song of Songs is in effect a celebration of that good condition, and as the Song comes to a close the word used to encapsulate this goodness is 'shalom' (8:10), which I take in this context to mean the full enjoyment of what our created natures naturally desire and long for (the NIV's 'contentment' is not an adequate translation). The NT teaching about singleness as a state which is preferable in certain circumstances (1 Cor. 7), or which may be embraced voluntarily for the sake of the kingdom of God (Jesus is the supreme example of this), is to be seen against this background. It does not conflict with it or overturn it. In other words, singleness remains a state that is 'not good' in the sense that it is a state of loneliness in which certain natural created desires are not met. There are compensations, of course, and important benefits, but particular needs remain unmet, and the single person has to live with that

The Song, the gospel and eschatology

In general, the New Testament takes the teaching of the Old Testament about male–female relationships and relates it to eschatology. The one-flesh union of man and woman remains good, and part of God's order for our created existence. But the ultimate peace/wholeness (shalom) is not to be found there, nor is the final return to Eden. Sex is good, but not the greatest good, and that is why it can be forgone, if need be, for the sake of the kingdom.[32] The true and final triumph over death and the grave, the complete release from the curse of the fall, is found in the cross of Christ, and in the new relationship between God and his people that it brings about. That relationship is depicted in gospel terms as a relationship between a bridegroom and his bride, and the final joy as a marriage.[33] According to Jesus, there will be no sex or marriage in heaven as we know them now (Matt. 22:30; Luke 20:35), but neither will there be any singleness, for both will have been replaced by a greater reality, the final union between Christ and his people, in which all of the redeemed will be included (Rev. 19:6–10). The Bible, like the Song of Songs, ends with a bride calling for the one who loves her to come (Rev. 22:17, 20; Song 8:14). So, from a New Testament perspective, the love depicted in the Song is not only a taste of what was given in creation, but a sign of what will be consummated in the new creation – a sign of the gospel.

> For this reason a man will leave his father and mother and be united to his wife, and the two shall become one flesh. This is a profound mystery – but I am talking about Christ and the church (Eph. 5:31–32).

At the most fundamental level, as we have seen, the Song of Songs is

---

fact and work through it. It is important to acknowledge this; otherwise there is a danger of moving into a kind of unreality and denial that are not helpful, either to single people themselves, or to those who minister to them. Cf. Richardson 1995.

[32] This is the basic principle that underlies Paul's teaching about marriage and singleness in 1 Cor. 7.

[33] As we have seen, the marriage relationship between Christ and the church has its antecedent, in terms of biblical theology, in the relationship between Yahweh and Israel in the OT. But the new covenant, inaugurated by the death and resurrection of Christ, creates a new people of God consisting of all who are 'in Christ', and places the marriage between God and his people on a new, firmer footing. By implication, of course, unfaithfulness to this relationship, in the NT as in the OT, is spiritual adultery. For a thorough treatment of this biblical theme see Ortlund 1996.

about the nature of love itself. It is in fact the only book of the Bible wholly devoted to this subject, and therefore has a special claim to be heard in any attempt to formulate a fully biblical view of it. Its special contribution is to underline the affective dimension of love. True love – love as strong as death – is not simply a matter of the mind or of the will, but of the affections as well. And that is true whether we speak of the love between a man and a woman, or that between Yahweh and Israel, or that between Christ and the church. To love God truly is not simply to keep his commandments, but to thirst for him as a deer thirsts for flowing streams (Ps. 42:1), and to long for him as a bride longs for her groom. For that is how we ourselves are loved by God,[34] and it is also how we are to love one another.[35] When what should be the fruits and accompaniments of love are mistaken for love itself, the heart sooner or later goes out of religion, however committed to orthodoxy and good works it may be, and it becomes a burden rather than a joy.

The Song of Songs is there to stop love going out of our relationships, with God and with one another. It is a splendid garment, to be worn not with awkwardness and embarrassment, but festively, with joy and deep thankfulness to him who gave it to us as Holy Scripture.

---

[34] Key statements about his saving acts in both OT and NT are prefaced by statements of his love; e.g. 'When Israel was a child, I loved him, and out of Egypt I called my son' (Hos. 11:1), 'God so loved the world that he gave his one and only Son' (John 3:16), 'Christ loved the church and gave himself up for her' (Eph. 5:25), or as Paul put it so personally, 'The Son of God ... loved me and gave himself for me' (Gal. 2:20). Most striking of all, perhaps, is Hosea's depiction of Yahweh struggling over his need to discipline Israel: 'How can I give you up, Ephraim? How can I hand you over, Israel? ... My heart is changed within me; all my compassion is aroused' (Hos. 11:8).

[35] E.g. Eph. 5:2, '... live a life of love, just as Christ loved us'; 1 Pet. 1:22, 'Now that you have purified yourselves by obeying the truth so that you have sincere love for your brothers, love one another deeply, from the heart.'

Chapter Two

Ruth
Garment of kindness

How precious is Your lovingkindness, O God!
Therefore the children of men put their trust
under the shadow of Your wings.
Psalm 36:7, NKJV

Ruth is a gentle book. It is so gentle that we are at first beguiled into thinking of it as merely heartwarming and reassuring, welcome relief from the turbulence of Judges or the emotional intensity of the Song of Songs. But the occasional ripple on the surface suggests that everything is not as it at first appears; that there is some turbulence in the depths. The apparent freedom with which the law is interpreted, the intermarriage with foreigners, and the admission of a Moabite into Israel, give this gentle idyll a surprisingly controversial edge. Furthermore, the connections with David and Bethlehem hint at a larger significance than the domestic setting and the charmingly simple plot at first suggest. I have called Ruth the 'scroll of kindness' for reasons that will be come apparent in due course. But if kindness is its theme, it is kindness of a radical and controversial sort; a kindness that makes ripples.

I
Ruth as a romantic comedy

The term 'romantic comedy' is probably too specialized and restrictive for Ruth.[1] But it is certainly 'romantic' inasmuch as it features courtship and marriage. And it is a 'comedy' in the sense that it has a happy ending. More generally it is a story – a short story or novella (so e.g. Larkin 1996: 9). This may seem too obvious to mention, but I have

[1] Ruth lacks the element of high adventure normally associated with romance literature, and it has a serious theological agenda not normally associated with comedy.

always believed that a willingness to start with the obvious is an essential element of good literary criticism. It is a form of epistemic humility, a willingness to submit to the text and to let it determine the shape of the interpretation; a readiness to be attentive, and to be led from the obvious design features of the text into its more subtle levels of meaning.

The charm and apparent simplicity of the story are in fact quite deceptive. Ruth has a finely articulated plot, and, as with all stories, the plot is its basic structural feature. Careful attention to its workings will be crucial for the identification of the themes. The overall movement is from death to life, barrenness to fruitfulness, emptiness to fullness, curse to blessing. And along the way there are many entertaining developments: Boaz's discreet but unmistakable courting of Ruth, the feminine scheming by Naomi to force Boaz's hand, his embarrassment at finding 'a woman' lying at his feet on the threshing-floor in the half-light of dawn, and his shrewd handling of the claims of the nearer kinsman in chapter 4, out of which the happy ending emerges.

Episodic structure

I use the term 'episode' here to refer to a more or less complete narrative movement. The story as a whole consists of four such episodes, corresponding roughly to the four chapters (cf. Larkin 1996: 42; Hubbard 1998: 74–75). The first traces Naomi's movement from Bethlehem in Judah to Moab and back again. Episodes 2 and 3, at the centre of the book, are structurally parallel. In both of them Ruth leaves Naomi in the morning, has an encounter with Boaz, and returns to her in the evening. In an article on the structure of Ruth, Stephen Bertman (1965: 165) has identified no fewer than five major matching elements in these two chapters:

Chapter 2	*Chapter 3*
1. Ruth asks Naomi if she can go, and tells her what she will do; Naomi bids her go.	1. Naomi bids Ruth go, and tells her what to do.
2. Ruth goes.	2. Ruth goes.
3. Boaz asks who Ruth is, and is told.	3. Boaz asks who Ruth is, and is told.
4. Boaz asks Ruth to stay,	4. Boaz says Ruth is

says she is worthy of being blessed, and gives her food.	worthy of being blessed, asks her to stay, and gives her food.
5. Ruth speaks to Naomi, tells her what has happened, and receives her counsel.	5. Ruth speaks to Naomi, tells her what has happened, and receives her counsel.

Only in items 1 and 4 are there any significant variations in the order in which corresponding elements occur.

The fourth episode is different from the other three in that there is no departure and return. Here instead the movement is linear, from the disposal of the competitor, to the union of Ruth and Boaz, to the birth of their child. Finally, with the genealogy at the end of the chapter, the story bursts its own horizon and opens out into the future.

With these preliminary observations, we are now in a position to explore each of the episodes in more detail, with particular reference to the way the characters are presented, how they develop and interact, and what issues emerge in the process.

Emptiness (1:1–22)

Departure

> [1]In the days when the judges ruled, there was a famine in the land, and a man from Bethlehem in Judah, together with his wife and two sons, went to live for a while in the country of Moab. [2]The man's name was Elimelech, his wife's name Naomi, and the names of his two sons were Mahlon and Kilion. They were Ephrathites from Bethlehem, Judah. And they went to Moab and lived there. [3]Now Elimelech, Naomi's husband, died, and she was left with her two sons. [4]They married Moabite women, one named Orpah and the other Ruth. After they had lived there about ten years, [5]both Mahlon and Kilion also died, and [the woman][2] was left without her two sons and her husband.

These first three verses are the seed from which the story will grow. They establish its general time-frame ('the days when the judges ruled'). They present a general problem to be solved ('there was a

---

[2] The NIV has 'Naomi'; the MT simply has 'the woman' (*hā 'iššâ*).

famine in the land'), and a more intense problem faced by one particular character (Naomi's personal destitution). The first problem is solved in 1:6, almost before the story gets under way. The second is not resolved until the end of the book, when Naomi cradles Obed in her arms (4:17). Clearly, then, the second problem is the real one; the first is simply the trigger for it to emerge. The story is about the reversal of Naomi's destitution.[3]

A striking feature of this opening paragraph is the pointed way in which all the characters are named, even those who will soon be removed and play no further part in the story: Elimelech, Mahlon, Kilion and Orpah. One of the names, and possibly at least one other, will turn out to be significant in themselves. What concerns us here, however, is the fact that there is *so much* naming at this point in the story. One effect of these personal names, together with the names of places such as Bethlehem, Judah and Moab, is to anchor the story in a more particular way into its space-time context. It is not about 'a certain man', as a parable might be, but this man, with this wife and these sons, who lived in this place, during the time of the judges. While this does not establish the historicity of the story, it certainly gives it a *connection* with history, especially when these names become linked, via the closing genealogy, with the figure of David. Second, by simply being where they are, these names are part of the literary artistry of the book. For if it begins with a cluster of names, that is also how it ends. This opening paragraph and the closing genealogy constitute a frame around the intervening narrative. Finally, the naming, in a negative way, contributes significantly to the depiction of Naomi's decline into destitution. As the 'while'[4] of 1:1 lengthens into the 'ten years' of 1:4, and family members die, so the naming falls away too, until Naomi is left at the end simply as *hā'iššâ*, 'the woman', bereft of 'her two sons and her husband', the unnamed ghosts of absent figures. It is as though Naomi has lost not only her family, but even her own name. That is the symbolic end point of her descent into emptiness.

Return

[19] So the two women went on until they came to Bethlehem. When they arrived in Bethlehem, the whole town was stirred

---

[3] Josephus (*Antiquities* 5.9.2) noted that the book of Ruth shows how God wonderfully lifts up the lowly and brings down the proud. Cf. Larkin 1996: 49.

[4] The MT has *wayyēlek ... lāgûr*, 'he went ... to sojourn'. The NIV's 'went to live for a while' accurately captures the sense.

because of them, and the women exclaimed, 'Can this be Naomi?'

[20] 'Don't call me Naomi,' she told them. 'Call me Mara, because the Almighty has made my life very bitter. [21] I went away full, but the LORD has brought me back empty. Why call me Naomi? The LORD has afflicted me; the Almighty has brought misfortune upon me.'

[22] So Naomi returned from Moab accompanied by Ruth the Moabitess, her daughter-in-law, arriving in Bethlehem as the barley harvest was beginning.

The first episode ends with Naomi's arrival back in Bethlehem. This marks the end of her physical return. But there is much more to her coming back than this, as her pregnant speech in verses 20–21 clearly indicates. She went away, but the LORD has brought her back. She went away full, but has been brought back empty, and in her own mind that emptiness is the result of discipline to which the Almighty has subjected her. She is no longer fit to be called Naomi ('sweet'), but should be called Mara ('bitter'). This opens a window on to the psychological plane of the story and strongly suggests that the departure and return are to be understood thematically in terms of rebellion and repentance. Naomi comes back from the far country as a returning prodigal.

Caution is needed here, for a particular character's perception of events cannot automatically be taken as coinciding with the narrator's, and therefore with the theme of the text as a whole. However, there are good reasons for thinking that here Naomi does in fact articulate the theme. The first is the sheer frequency with which the verb šûḇ, 'to return, turn back', is used in this chapter. It occurs no fewer than twelve times.[5] In verse 6 Naomi and her daughters-in-law prepare to return; in verse 7 they set out to return; in verses 8–10 Naomi tells the two girls to 'go, return' to their mother's home, but they decline, and insist instead on returning with Naomi. In verses 12–15 she urges them again, 'Return ... Go', and when Orpah does so, Naomi encourages Ruth to return after her. But in verse 16 Ruth begs Naomi not to make her return. And in the last verse of the chapter Naomi and Ruth are found united in returning. Naomi returns, with Ruth the Moabitess, her daughter-in-law, literally 'the one who returned'.[6] The frequency of the

---

[5] In 1:1, 7, 8, 10, 11, 12 (twice), 16, 21 and 22 (twice). Larkin (1996: 42) notes that it is a catchword that helps to give cohesion to the chapter.

[6] Cf. Larkin (1996: 49): 'Even Ruth is said to "return", notwithstanding that she is a

usage of 'return' is far beyond the requirements of a simple account of a return journey. And this takes on a particular significance when it is recognized that *šûḇ* is the term regularly used in the prophets for repentance.

The second indication that Naomi's speech at this point is of particular significance is the way the circumstances of her return are described. It is not simply her destitution which brings her back, but hearing, in the land of Moab, that 'the LORD [has] come to the aid of his people by providing food for them' (1:6). This creates a great sense of distance between Naomi and her homeland, and between her and the LORD and his people. The provision which is spoken of here is a covenanted provision, which Naomi is at present missing out on because she has forsaken the covenant community. Her return is a choice to identify with that community again. It is a return, not just to Bethlehem, but to Yahweh and Yahweh's people. Ruth, her daughter-in-law, has never been part of that community except through marriage. Orpah, who acts as her foil in this episode, acts out the alternative which is open to Ruth; she returns to her own gods and her own people. But Ruth decides very deliberately not to do this. Her decision to return with Naomi is a choice to commit herself irrevocably, not just to Naomi, but to the God and the people to whom Naomi herself is returning (1:16).

It is entirely in keeping with this repentance theme that Naomi comes back without any element of self-justification. On the face of it, her leaving was entirely reasonable. There was famine in Bethlehem, and she was a mother with a family to feed. In any case, the decision does not appear to have been hers, or at least not primarily hers. The active subject in 1:1 is Elimelech, not Naomi. She was the wife of a man who went away. But in her speech as she returns, all extenuating circumstances are ignored, and she takes the whole responsibility on herself with the unadorned confession, 'I went away' (1:21).

Nevertheless, her psychological condition is fragile rather than robust. This is hinted at in the play on her name; she is 'bitter'.[7] It is

---

foreigner ... as if she represents the reintegration of one of the lines issuing from Lot back into Israel.'

[7] There is an objective aspect to her bitterness in the bereavement, dislocation and poverty that have come upon her. The Almighty has made her life bitter (1:20). But there is also a subjective aspect, a bitterness she feels. There is a suggestion of this in the ambiguity of 1:13, which is either 'It is more bitter for me than for you' (NIV), or 'It is exceedingly bitter to me for your sake' (RSV). The MT has *mar-lî mᵉ'ōḏ mikkem*, where the *min* is either comparative ('more than') or prepositional ('because of').

also seen in the way she speaks of the treatment she has received at God's hand: 'the LORD's hand has gone out against me' (1:13), 'the Almighty has made my life very bitter' (1:20), 'the LORD has brought me back empty', and 'the Almighty has brought misfortune upon me' (1:21).[8] One can hardly fail to detect elements of accusation and self-pity here. In that sense her repentance is flawed, and her perception of her condition distorted by self-absorption. For does she really come back empty? The word 'empty' values her loyal daughter-in-law (who has forsaken everything to follow her, and pledged undying loyalty to her) as nothing, perhaps even as an embarrassment, the one remaining evidence of her entanglement with Moab which she has failed to shake off (cf. Fewell & Gunn 1990: 28–29). Little does she know that that same daughter-in-law will play a key role in her rehabilitation.

One final observation before we leave this first episode. The theme of 'kindness' (ḥeseḏ) makes its first appearence here, though with no indication of the rich development it will receive later. Naomi recognizes that Orpah and Ruth have shown 'kindness' to their Jewish husbands and to herself during their time in Moab. And she encourages them to go back by expressing hope that Yahweh may reward them by providing them with new husbands there (1:8–9). 'Kindness' here is essentially acceptance of the duty of care involved in covenanted relationships, especially those of marriage and family. By extension, Yahweh is expected to show reciprocal kindness to those who have acted in this way towards members of his own covenant community. In this latter case, kindness is a form of reward. It is striking that Naomi expects no such kindness to be extended to herself, or to her daughters-in-law if they return with her. As far as she can see, their marriage prospects in Israel would be be nil (1:11–13). She herself presumably expects to be able to survive in Bethlehem; otherwise she would not return at all. But she anticipates nothing deserving the name of kindness, least of all from Yahweh. She seems blind to Ruth's continuing kindness to her, and to the promise that it holds.

But although Naomi cannot presently see beyond it, the end of this episode is also a beginning. The two destitute women arrive in Bethlelem at the start of the barley harvest (1:22).

Seeking (2:1–23)

After the emptiness of the first episode come two symbols of fullness,

---

[8] The chiasm, 'the LORD ... the Almighty ... the Almighty ... the LORD', is part of the artistry of the speech.

or plenty. The first is the harvest itself; the second is the impressive figure of Boaz, whose harvest it is. He is a 'man of standing' ('*îš gibbôr ḥayil*), and 'a relative' (*môḏaʻ*) of Naomi's husband (2:1), both pregnant expressions on which we will have cause to reflect further. Enter the rich relative; here surely are the materials for a fruitful development of the plot! And into this scene of plenty ventures Ruth. Naomi is still too depressed to take the action that is required, so the initiative passes to Ruth,[9] and Naomi retires into the background. This episode belongs essentially to Boaz and Ruth.

The theme of kindness continues here, as we shall observe in a moment. But now it is more richly nuanced by the explicit presence of other, related concepts. Boaz speaks of reward: 'May the LORD repay you for what you have done. May you be richly rewarded by the LORD, the God of Israel' (2:12). But Ruth, acutely aware of her vulnerability, speaks of 'grace' or 'favour': 'Why have I found such favour [*ḥēn*] in your eyes that you should notice me – a foreigner? ... May I continue to find favour [*ḥēn*] in your eyes, my lord' (2:10, 13). Binding these two together is the hint of obligation inherent in family ties, and the duty of care, especially to the foreigner, that comes with the possession of wealth. And a special quality is given to all this, of course, by the fact that Boaz is a man and Ruth a young woman.

Boaz is presented as a pious Israelite, with a fine sense of his obligations and a readiness to accept them. He also seems to be aware that not all Israelite men are as he is. He orders his men not to 'touch' Ruth (2:9), and warns her not to go elsewhere, 'because in someone else's field you might be harmed' (2:22). All is not sweetness and light in this pastoral scene; dark threats lurk in the wings. Against this background Boaz acts as Ruth's provider and protector. He allows her to glean in his field, gives her food and water, draws her in from the margins to the centre of the social group he superintends, and sends her home with plenty to share with Naomi. There is a generosity here that borders on extravagance; he even instructs his men to pull out some stalks from the sheaves for Ruth to gather (2:16). It may be nothing more than true piety; Boaz observes the spirit of the law, not just its letter. But it may also be right that we see more in his actions does than Boaz himself sees, or perhaps *allows* himself to see at this stage. At any rate, this is kindness that is not mere compliance with legal obligation; it is a far richer kindness than that.

All this is pulled together, and set in a larger, theological framework, as Ruth returns to Naomi and the episode draws to a close. Naomi is

---

[9] We are prepared for her to play this role by her decisiveness in ch. 1.

suddenly and marvellously aroused from her emotional torpor by the news that Ruth has met Boaz, for Naomi knows something about him that Ruth does not, and of which we ourselves have seen only a glimmer before this. Boaz is not just a relative, but a 'close' relative, or 'kinsman-redeemer' (a *gō'ēl*, 2:20). It is one of those crystallizing moments in a story when the plot changes gear, and latent possibilities suddenly rise to the surface. For Naomi is aware of the special obligations that devolve on a *gō'ēl* in Israelite law and custom.[10] She is energized by hope, and suddenly able to see, not only her circumstances, but God himself, in a new light, which she distils in a double blessing:

[19] 'Blessed be the man who took care of you ...
[20] 'Blessed be he by the LORD ... who has not abandoned his kindness (*ḥeseḏ*) towards the living and the dead.' She added, 'That man is closely related to us; he is one of our kinsmen-redeemers (*gō'ēl*)' (my translation).

D. F. Rauber (1970: 32–33) has captured the significance of these words beautifully: 'With the advent of ... understanding comes an upward surge of her spirit, a lifting from the depths ... and we know that Naomi, who herself was among the dead, now lives again.'

In the kindness of Boaz Naomi perceives the kindness of Yahweh, and knows herself to be the object of it. She is right, of course, but needed to say it much more for her own sake than for ours. For what she has just heard by way of report, we have observed as it gradually unfolded. Was it by pure chance that Ruth 'found herself' working in a field belonging to Boaz (2:3), or that 'just then'[11] Boaz himself arrived from Bethlehem (2:4a)? The fact that the name of Yahweh is found almost at once on Boaz's lips (2:4b), and continues to occur in greetings and blessings in the following verses, provides the implicit answer. The revelation that Boaz is a *gō'ēl* (2:20b) is simply the capstone of a thematic structure the author has been erecting throughout the whole course of the episode: Boaz, lord of the harvest, with Ruth as his partner, is the chosen means of filling Naomi's emptiness. The grain Ruth brings to her as she returns is the earnest of what is to come. Boaz himself, we suspect, already has an inkling of his destiny. To quote Rauber again, 'all that remains is to draw what Boaz partially knows into the full light of consciousness' (1970: 33).

---

[10] See Lev. 25:25–28; Num. 35:6–28; Deut. 19:4–13.
[11] The MT has the emphatic particle *hinnēh*.

Finding (3:1–18)

After harvest comes threshing, and with it the resumption of the initiative by Naomi, who is now ready for action. Episode 3 begins with her announcing her intention to seek 'rest' – marriage and a home – for Ruth. It ends with her expressing strong confidence that Boaz will not 'rest' until the matter is settled.[12] It is about a movement towards rest, an initiative that brings Ruth and Naomi to the brink of realizing the potential that the previous episode offered, as threshing realizes the potential of harvest. For rest, especially in the form of marriage and home, is another figure for fullness. We have already noted some broad structural parallels between this episode and the previous one. But the relationship is one of contrast and development rather than mere repetition.

With Ruth's movement to the threshing-floor in verse 6, the second and central scene of the episode is opened. She speaks only when she is spoken to (3:9), following Naomi's instructions exactly (3:5). The contrast at this point with the corresponding scene in chapter 2 is striking. Ruth no longer refers to her foreignness, or to the fact that she is not one of Boaz's workers. On the contrary, she identifies herself now as 'Ruth your maidservant' (3:9a, my translation). A new intimacy is being claimed and expressed here in word and action. Her tone is deferential, but she presses her claim pointedly by addressing Boaz directly as her *gō'ēl* (3:9b). Precisely what she expects of him has already been expressed by her uncovering of his legs; it is now made even plainer by the request, 'Spread your skirt (literally "wing") over me' (3:9, my translation; cf. Ezek. 16:8). In the previous episode Boaz had expressed the wish that Yahweh, under whose 'wings' Ruth had come to take refuge (2:12), would richly reward her. It was a precious moment, with Boaz poised delicately between recognition and reserve. Now Ruth challenges him to translate his pious words into action by being the means by which the blessing will be fulfilled.

What brings Boaz from reserve to willingness and decision is his increasing appreciation of Ruth's character, which he now describes in words which unwittingly link him with her. We have noted how the narrator introduced Boaz to us in 2:1 as 'a man of standing', an *'îš gibbôr ḥayil*. Boaz now tells Ruth that all his fellow-townsmen acknowledge that she is 'a woman of noble character' (3:11), an *'ēšet*

---

[12] The MT has the noun *mānôaḥ* in 3:1 (NIV 'a home') and the verb *šqṭ* (Qal imperfect) in 3:18. The semantic range of the two roots is virtually identical.

ḥayil. It is in this significant context that the theme of 'kindness' resurfaces, and is brought into direct contact with the emerging relationship between them. Boaz again:

> [10] '[Yahweh] bless you, my daughter ... This kindness [*ḥeseḏ*] is greater than that which you showed earlier.'

Far from resenting Ruth's request as an unwelcome imposition, Boaz regards it as a kindness, greater even than her kindness to Naomi. If there is a nobility of character that Boaz and Ruth have in common, the term 'kindness' (*ḥeseḏ*) distills the essence of it.

Why Boaz should regard Ruth's proposal as a great kindness is at one level obvious; it answers the unspoken desire of his own heart and brings him release. That can now be taken for granted. But it also carries with it the first hint of a complication which is about to cast a cloud over all this happy prospect. It is a kindness because there were, and are, alternatives – other men, younger than Boaz,[13] who also know of Ruth's fine qualities, and whom Ruth could have approached with hope of success (3:10–11). In mentioning these men, however, Boaz is simply edging towards a disclosure which he dreads, but knows must be made: the existence of one particular man whose interest in Ruth must be reckoned with. There is a kinsman (a *gō'ēl*) nearer than Boaz himself (3:12).

In fact, all of this talk about Ruth choosing him above others is something of a conceit on Boaz's part. For in reality it is Naomi rather than Ruth who has done the choosing. And it is Naomi who has been aware of other possibilities, an awareness we can now recognize in her earlier words, 'he [Boaz] is *one* of our kinsman-redeemers' (2:20, my emphasis). But in calling Ruth's act a kindness, Boaz indirectly declares his love for her and encourages her to make the choice her own – and to hold to it in the face of the disclosure he now feels bound to make. It is another element in his wooing of her. It also shows us an aspect of Boaz's character that will be displayed more fully in the final episode. If Boaz is noble, he is also shrewd.

The night scene at the threshing-floor is handled delicately, and with an apparent concern to avoid any suggestion of sexual misconduct. The possibility of scandal certainly exists, and is implicitly acknowledged by Boaz's directive that no-one should know of the visit (3:14).[14] But

---

[13] 'From Boaz's reference to "young men" (iii 10) it may clearly be inferred that he was no longer young himself' (Beattie 1977: 193).

[14] According to Josephus, Boaz bade Ruth, at daybreak, to 'take as much of the barley

the only misconduct of which they could justly be accused is of pursuing their relationship so far without first consulting the nearer kinsman. The meeting at the threshing-floor has made this matter urgent, and so created the momentum for the opening scene of the next episode.

One final comment, however, before leaving this present one. Ruth returns to Naomi loaded with six measures of barley that Boaz has placed in her shawl (3:15). Of particular interest are his words as he hands this bounty to her: 'You must not go back to your mother-in-law empty' (*rêqam*, 3:17, my translation). It is as though he had heard Naomi's bitter words back in 1:21, 'The LORD has brought me back empty [*rêqam*]', and the slur that they were on Ruth. Boaz fills Naomi's emptiness, but he fills Ruth's as well.

Fullness (4:1–22)

The emptiness/fullness theme receives its final, climactic outworking in the second half of this episode, from 4:11 onwards. The opening scene, at the city gate,[15] is properly an interlude, and a prelude to the climax of the story rather than part of it. We shall return to it later when we look in a more considered way at the wider Old Testament context. Here we simply note four things in passing.

First, this scene reinforces the presentation of Boaz as a 'man of standing' (*'îš gibbôr ḥayil*, 2:1), by showing the respect he commands at the city gate. Secondly, it continues the pattern of happy coincidence which suggests God's providential ordering of events. No sooner has Boaz taken his seat in the gate than the man he had mentioned 'happens' to come along (4:1).[16] Thirdly, as we have already noted, it gives further insight into the blend of nobility and shrewdness in Boaz's character, especially in the way he deals with the potential threat posed by this man. And finally, by prolonging suspense, it contributes indirectly to the profoundly satisfying character of the climax that follows. Because of this scene, the union of Boaz and Ruth becomes not simply a consummation, but a triumph.

The climax itself is a complex one, and identifying its centre (the climax within the climax) depends to some extent on whether we

---

as she could carry and be off to her mother-in-law before anyone could see that she had slept there, since it is wise to guard against scandal of that kind and the more so when nothing had passed'. Cited in Beattie 1977: 180.

[15] Note the anticipation of this in 3:11, literally 'all the gate of my people know ...'

[16] *Hinnēh* is used, as in 2:4, where it is Boaz's propitious arrival that is noted.

understand Ruth or Naomi to be the principal character. The climax of the Ruth–Boaz strand of the plot comes in 4:13: 'So Boaz took Ruth and she became his wife ... and she gave birth to a son.' The climax of Naomi's story is in 4:16–17: 'Then Naomi took the child, laid him in her lap and cared for him. The women living there said, "Naomi has a son"'. But then, beyond these, emerges a climax which may, in a sense, be seen to surpass both of them: 'And they named him Obed. He was the father of Jesse, the father of David' (4:17). With that, however, we have passed beyond the story itself to its wider setting. David is not a participant in the story, but the rationale for it, the reason it has been told at all. The significance of Ruth and Naomi is to be found ultimately in their connection with David. But the story itself is theirs essentially, and their shared fullness is its true climax.

Both elements of this climax are accompanied by a blessing that interprets it. In 4:11–12, Ruth and Boaz are blessed by the elders:

> [11] May the LORD make the woman who is coming into your home like Rachel and Leah, who together built up the house of Israel. May you have standing in Ephrathah and be famous in Bethelehem. [12] Through the offspring the LORD gives you by this young woman, may your family be like that of Perez, whom Tamar bore to Judah.'

Again, there are features to which we shall have to return. To be noted here is the double invocation of the name Yahweh (the LORD), and the linking of Boaz and Ruth with the great figures of Israel's patriarchal past. All the hints of divine providence noted earlier are now drawn together and summarized under the figure of Yahweh the builder. As he built up Israel through the patriarchs, so he is continuing to build it up through the union of Boaz and Ruth. What we have here may be a conventional wedding blessing, but if so the genealogy at the end of the chapter gives it a heightened significance in this case. The building Yahweh has been doing here has had David in view.

In contrast, the blessing the women pronounce on Naomi and Obed is much more focused on the personal and domestic aspects of the story.

> [14] 'Praise be to the LORD, who this day has not left you without a kinsman-redeemer [gō'ēl]. May he become famous throughout Israel! [15] He will renew your life and sustain you in your old age. For your daughter-in-law, who loves you and who is better to you than seven sons, has given him birth.

Virtually every phrase here resonates with the themes we have been tracing through the story. Boaz has been a kinsman-redeemer to Naomi, and a nearer one has made a brief appearance. But now this theme is focused down and brought to rest finally in the baby who lies in Naomi's lap. Obed is the final element in the filling of Naomi's emptiness. He will renew her life and sustain her in her old age, and he is Yahweh's gift to her. Indeed, Yahweh has not left her without a kinsman-redeemer.

But neither has Ruth; Obed, after all, is *her* baby first of all. She is included in the blessing, of course, but, rather sadly, it is the watching women who have to rescue her from neglect. At the beginning of the story Naomi was too consumed by her bitterness to acknowledge Ruth's presence; here she is too satiated with her contentment. Against this background, the closing words of the blessing are in effect a mild rebuke to Naomi. The silent daughter-in-law by her side is worth more to her than seven sons – a remarkable statement in a society where sons were valued so highly. Obed fills Ruth's emptiness as well as Naomi's by finally establishing her true worth, even if Naomi is slow to recognize it. It is Ruth who has given Obed birth, and so, in her own way, given Naomi a redeemer. Rauber is here worth quoting at length:

> ... looking back we see ... that the author has planted foreshadowings of this final scene in the intervening chapters. The reminder in chapter 2 is slight and glancing; it occurs when Ruth returns to Naomi from the fields with the fruit of her labour: 'and *she brought forth, and gave to her* that she had reserved after she was sufficed' (18). The same symbolic preview of birth and presentation is given more directly in chapter 3. Boaz has filled the apron of Ruth with grain, saying, 'These six measures of barley he gave me; for he said to me, *Go not empty unto thy mother in law*' (17). Thus the beginning and end of the thematic development are firmly linked; thus all the themes and figures come together and are fused in splendour and tenderness (1970: 35).

It is here in this final blessing that the word 'love' is used for the first and only time in the story: 'your daughter in law, who loves you (*'ăhēḇatek*)' (4:15). The characteristic term for describing the loyal, caring relationships between the characters in the story, as we have seen, has been 'kindness' (*ḥeseḏ*) – the kindness of Orpah and Ruth to their husbands, and of Ruth, in particular, to Naomi; the kindness of

Boaz to Ruth, and of Ruth to Boaz; and the kindness of Yahweh to them all. It is kindness which has had an element of legal obligation to it, but at the same time has gone beyond it. This kindness, which goes beyond the letter to the spirit of the law, is seen in Boaz's kindness to Ruth, where love is clearly involved, though the term is never used. What the climax does is to point us to the supreme example of kindness suffused by love in this story – at least, on the human level. And it locates it, somewhat unexpectedly, not in the understandable – and in that sense natural – love between a man and a woman, but in the extraordinary love of a foreigner, a young Moabitess, for her aged Israelite mother-in-law, who never fully appreciates it. At the same time, it merges the human and divine planes of the story together by encapsulating this insight in a blessing invoked in Yahweh's name, whose providence is the ultimate source of all that has come to pass. Here indeed is a supernatural, loving kindness, to be wondered at.

II

The book of Ruth is bound into its Old Testament context at many levels. We have already noted in passing the references to the patriarchs and David, to the period of the judges, and to the Torah prescriptions concerning gleaning. Most scholarly attention has been focused on five matters: the nature of Ruth's marriage and its relationship to the levirate-marriage legislation of Deuteronomy 25; the disposal of Naomi's land (an important part of the marriage negotiations) and its connection with the law of redemption in Leviticus 25; the apparent conflict between the story of Ruth and the ban on Moabites in Deuteronomy 23; the possible relationship between Ruth and the ban on marriage with foreign women (including Moabites) in Ezra's reforms (Ezra 10); and the implications of these and other matters for determining the date and the purpose of the book.[17] The issues are too numerous and complex to be addressed in detail here, and would in any case divert us somewhat from our purpose. The part of the book which has been the subject of most intense interest for study of this kind, the first part of chapter 4, is of relatively minor significance for the development of the book's themes, as we have seen. Furthermore, our particular concern is to identify how the book participates in the wider themes and theology of the Old

---

[17] See the review of the various proposals regarding the purpose of Ruth in Larkin 1996: 52–56.

Testament rather than to reconstruct its original setting and purpose. I shall refer to the above matters so far as they are relevant to our brief, but major on three issues which I judge to be of major literary and theological significance: Ruth's location in the canon, Ruth as salvation history, and Ruth and the law (including its traditional association with the Feast of Weeks).

Location in the canon

Ruth has been one of the most mobile books in the canon, being found in various positions before finally settling among the five *Megilloth*, or festival Scrolls.

The basic facts are helpfully summarized by Campbell (1972: 32–36) in the introduction to his Anchor Bible commentary on the book. Two basic traditions are reflected in the relevant sources, and it is difficult to determine which is earlier. The first places Ruth in the Prophets, immediately after Judges, as in the Septuagint. The same tradition appears to be reflected in Josephus, who holds that there are twenty-two canonical books (*Against Appion* 1.8), apparently requiring Ruth to be counted with Judges, and Lamentations with Jeremiah. The second places Ruth among the Writings, and has a number of variants within it. The fourth book of *Esdras*, from about the same time as Josephus, reckons the number of the canonical books as twenty-four, allowing Ruth and Lamentations to have an independent status. This accords with the Babylonian Talmud, which states the order of the Writings and puts Ruth first, ahead of Psalms and the wisdom books. There is widespread agreement that this order precedes the placing of Ruth among the five Scrolls (in the middle of the Writings), probably between the sixth and ninth centuries AD. The order of the Scrolls in editions of the Hebrew Bible before 1937 reflects the order of their use in connection with the relevant five festivals: the Songs of Songs at Passover, Ruth at Tabernacles, and so on. But the Leningrad codex on which *Biblica Hebraica* is based, from 1008 or 1009 AD, has a variation even on this, with Ruth as the first of the Scrolls, immediately after Proverbs, probably on chronological rather than on liturgical grounds. So even at the end of the process there still seems to have been some disagreement about what considerations should determine its precise location.

The book's search for a resting-place in a sense mirrors Ruth's own search. Its movements are of interest to us here because they provide important clues to how it was perceived to relate to its canonical context. The view which puts it among the Prophets, after Judges, associates it with the salvation-history traditions of the Old Testament. The placement in the Writings associates it with the worship and wisdom traditions. More particularly, placing it at the beginning of the Writings, before Psalms, makes it a kind of introduction to David, the great patron of Israel's liturgical tradition. The location after Proverbs implies that Ruth is the supreme example in the Old Testament of the 'noble woman' (*'ēšet ḥayil*) who is the subject of the acrostic poem of Proverbs 31 (cf. Campbell 1972: 34). The cumulative effect of all this is to underline how fully Ruth participates in the discourse of the Old Testament. We will now examine a couple of aspects of this in more detail.

Ruth as salvation history

The book of Ruth is spliced into the thread of salvation history at both ends, by the way it opens and the way it closes. And we have already noted above how the announcement of marriage and birth in 4:13 is framed by references to the glories of the past and the still greater glories to come (cf. Rauber 1970: 34). Ruth is as much a part of Old Testament salvation history as David himself is. But here we encounter something of an anomaly, for it contains no miraculous interventions by God, no inspired prophetic interpreters or spokespersons, and no events involving Israel as a whole. The story is entirely domestic and local in character, and the divine workings in it are hidden and providential; they lie beneath the surface rather than on it.

So the book of Ruth expands and deepens the concept of salvation history. It shows us that salvation history is continuous and not intermittent, and is just as really being advanced when miracles are absent as when they are present. It shows us that those whom God saves by signs and wonders, as at the exodus, he continues to save by his providential workings in their day-to-day lives, and that his kindness (*ḥeseḏ*), by which Israel is built up, is to be found not only in great national deliverances, but in the way his covenant people treat one another on a daily basis. It is micro, as opposed to macro, salvation history. There are points of connection here with the Joseph story, and especially with the book of Esther, which we shall look at in a later chapter.

Ruth and the law

That there are points of connection between the book of Ruth and the Torah (especially certain parts of Deuteronomy and Leviticus) is generally recognized. But the nature of the connections is hotly disputed, and depends to some extent on how one dates the documents. Does Ruth represent a later, flexible application of the provisions of the relevant lawcodes, or are the laws a later tightening up of earlier practices reflected in Ruth? Put in these terms, the arguments become circular and can never finally be resolved.

More to the point for our purposes here is the question how the book of Ruth functions in relation to the Torah *canonically*. Of what theological significance is it that, whatever its precise location, Ruth follows the Torah in the canon? And the starting-point in that question must be that Ruth functions, in part at least, as a study in the application of the Mosaic Torah to the daily life of the people of God. In fact that, in a sense, is how the whole of the Prophets and the Writings function, but the book of Ruth particularly so.

In matters such as provision for gleaning, or redemption of property, the law is observed meticulously, even extravagantly. The levirate (brother-in-law) marriage legislation of Deuteronomy 25, however, if it is on view at all, appears to be interpreted quite flexibly. Finally, and most controversially, at least one particular stipulation – the ban on Moabites ever entering the assembly of Yahweh (Deut. 23:3–6) – appears not to be observed at all! Nor can this matter be regarded as an issue of which the writer is ignorant, or to which he is indifferent, since he draws our attention to the fact that Ruth is a 'Moabitess' no fewer than six times in the book, distributed over three of its four chapters.[18] This concerned the rabbis so much that it gave rise to the explanation that Boaz, whom they identified as the judge Ibzan, had published a new law which stipulated that while the Torah excluded Moabites, this applied only to men – 'Moabite but not Moabitess' (*Ruth Rabbah* 2:10). This is at odds, though, with the way the same law is understood in Nehemiah 13:1, 23.

Rowley's (1965: 177–179) distinction between law and custom is helpful here.[19] Life is always more complex than law alone can handle,

[18] Ruth 1:22; 2:2, 6, 21; 4:5, 10. 'Moab' (and hence, by implication, Ruth's background) is mentioned a further six times, at 1:1, 2, 6, 22; 2:6; 4:3.

[19] Rowley, however, thinks that the law of Deut. 25:5–10 (concerning levirate marriage) reflects a limitation of the earlier, more flexible custom found in the book of Ruth and elsewhere. My own view is that the custom reflected in the book of Ruth

and what we see in Ruth is custom that reflects the spirit if not the letter of the law, and in doing so distinguishes between its lesser and weightier matters. Ruth is a Moabitess, but she is also a widow and a landless alien who has taken refuge under Yahweh's wings. And the author of Ruth apparently takes the view that, in such a case, it would be inappropriate to invoke the ban on Moabites. This ban on Moabites was no more intended to exclude someone like Ruth than the ban on Canaanites was intended to exclude someone like Rahab, and, if we are to take the tone of the book as a guide, Boaz is regarded as a model of law-*keeping* rather than of law-*breaking*. In other words, the book identifies the 'spirit' of the law as 'kindness' (*hesed*), or more specifically, '*loving*-kindness' – kindness with the excess and richness of love. In this Ruth is at one with the prophets, especially Micah who in this respect speaks for them all:

> He has showed you, O man, what is good;
>   and what does the LORD require of you?
> but to do justice, and to love kindness [*'ªhªbat ḥeseḏ*][20]
>   and to walk humbly with your God?

(Mic. 6:8, RSV)

In this context, the liturgical connection of Ruth with the Feast of Weeks takes on a particular significance. For apart from its traditional association with the barley harvest (Deut. 16:9), this is the feast that particularly commemorates the giving of the law to Israel, fifty days or seven weeks after the exodus from Egypt.[21] If to read the Song of Songs at Passover is to be reminded that redemption is an act of love, to read Ruth at Weeks is to be reminded that love – loving-*kindness* – is the fulfilling of the law.

III

What the New Testament does is to take the genealogy of David that

---

follows the Deuteronomic law and is in effect a case study in the application of it in a particular, complex situation. Whatever the merits of these particular views, the difference between custom and law needs to be recognized. The reality is that custom both precedes and follows law.

[20] The NIV has 'to love mercy'.

[21] This connection was explicitly made from the intertestamental period onwards. *Jubilees* 1:1; 4:17; TB *Pesaḥîm* 68b; Midrash *Tanḥuma* 26c. Cf. Freeman 1996.

closes the book of Ruth and reproduce its contents in the genealogies of Jesus in Matthew 1 and Luke 3. This is of profound theological significance, because it brings the book of Ruth, with its distinctive themes, into explicit connection with that salvation history which is now seen to have its fulfilment in the coming of Christ, the great Son of David and the Messiah. It tells us that the loving-kindness that fulfils the law is to be found supremely here, in the birth of Jesus and the saving events that flow from it. The theme of salvation in Christ as the supreme kindness is taken further in the epistles, and crystallized by Paul especially in an apparent word-play, where he speaks of the incomparable riches of God's grace, expressed in his kindness to us (*en chrēstotēti*) in Christ Jesus (*en Christō*) (Eph. 2:7; cf. Titus 3:4).

As far as the particulars of the New Testament genealogies are concerned, the only significant variation from Ruth 4 is in the explicit linking of Boaz with Ruth his wife and Rahab his mother (Matt. 1:5).[22] This occurs only in Matthew, and is in accord with a larger theological construct that spans the whole of Matthew's Gospel. Matthew begins by identifying Jesus as 'the son of David, the son of Abraham' (1:1), and concludes with the Great Commission to take the gospel to 'all nations' (28:19). There are strong indications here that Matthew sees Jesus' mission against the backdrop of the Abrahamic covenant, with its promise of blessing for all nations. This is confirmed by other features of his Gospel which we cannot treat in detail here, but which include the distinctive Magi passage of chapter 2 and the setting of the beginning of Jesus' preaching ministry in 'Galilee of the Gentiles' in chapter 4.

The mention of Ruth and Rahab in the genealogy of Matthew 1 links the 'kindness' theme of Ruth to this broader construct. By their association with Boaz the redeemer, these two Gentile women are incorporated not only into Israel, but also into David and into Christ. This adds a particular dimension to the theme of kindness as it relates to salvation history. The kindness of God displayed in the book of Ruth is a kindness that not only builds up Israel, but draws in the Gentiles to share in her covenant blessings. In this way, too, Ruth throws light on an aspect of the gospel that comes to full expression in the New Testament, as Matthew seems to be at pains to show us.

The explicit connections the New Testament makes with the book of Ruth are in the area of what we might call salvation history in the strong sense. However, other aspects of the book's teaching also lie at

---

[22] Other departures from the standard form of the bibliography include the references to Tamar (v. 3), and Bathsheba, 'Uriah's wife' (v. 6).

the heart of the New Testament exposition of the gospel. When Paul says that 'in all things God works for the good of those who love him, who have been called according to his purpose' (Rom. 8:28), he is giving expression to the theme of 'providential salvation', or 'ongoing, continuous salvation', that we found in Ruth. Jesus' summary of the law as love of God and neighbour captures the essence of what Ruth teaches about loving-kindness being the fulfilment of the law in the ethical sense. And finally, when the New Testament enjoins 'kindness' (*chrēstotēs*) on us as a leading Christian virtue, a fruit of the Spirit and part of our imitation of Christ (Gal. 5:22; Eph. 4:32), it does by way of direct exhortation what Ruth does more subtly in narrative form.

'Kindness' is an incidental theme in the New Testament, but it is woven into the whole texture of Ruth from beginning to end. Ruth is, supremely, the scroll of kindness, as the Song of Songs is the scroll of love. It, too, is to be worn festally, in celebration of the kindness that has been shown to us. But it is also to be worn quietly, with awe and humility, for to put on kindness is to clothe ourselves with the very character of God himself.

Chapter Three

Lamentations
Garment of suffering

Learning is our soul's requirement,
and suffering our most persuasive teacher.
Ruadh of Kells [1]

At this point we move forward approximately two months in the Jewish
sacred calendar to the month of Ab, corresponding roughly to July-
August, and with that we come to a very different kind of festival and a
markedly different kind of scroll. Lamentations is the scroll which is
read at the Ninth of Ab, an annual day of fasting and mourning which
commemorates the destruction of the Jerusalem temple in 587 BC, and
(in modern times) all other disasters that have befallen the Jews, right
down to and including the Holocaust. If the Song of Songs is the
supreme song, Lamentations is the eternal lament of the Jewish people.

The fast of the Ninth of Ab is not directly instituted in Scripture, but
the events that gave rise to it certainly are. The facts concerning the
destruction of Jerusalem and its temple by Nebuchadnezzar's forces are
given in summary form in 2 Kings 25:1–21. But what is described there
so prosaically and dispassionately is revisited in Lamentations in a way
that allows the pain to surface and find appropriate expression. It is
possible that at least some of the material now included in the book had
its origins in public mourning rites that were held at the site of the
ruined temple from earliest times (Jer. 41:5; Zech. 7:3, 5; 8:19).

The contrast between this scroll and the preceding two could scarcely
be more striking. From the sunny heights of love and kindness we are
drawn down here into a dark shaft of tragic loss and acute anguish.
There was pain, of course, in the first two scrolls, but it was confined to
unsettling moments, or was there as a background that steadily receded
as joy took hold. Here it is the total environment in which people are
immersed, all-encompassing, dark and suffocating. Under its pressure

---

[1] In Stephen Lawhead's novel, *Byzantium* (London: HarperCollins, 1997), p. 632.
Ruadh is assistant to the Abbot of the monastery at Kells, and confessor to Alden, who is
the hero of the story.

the bonding relationships that give wholeness to life collapse, or are savagely reversed. There is no comforter; priests and prophets grope their way through the streets like blind men, and mothers devour their own children. Everyone is alone, and worst of all, Yahweh himself has become an enemy. We have arrived at one of the darkest moments of Israel's history.

I

Lamentations as 'ordered grief'

It is somewhat startling to discover that a book that portrays such radical disorientation should be one of the most ordered works in the Old Testament. But that is in fact what Lamentations is. Each of the five chapters contains one poem of twenty-two verses, except for chapter 3, which has sixty-six. The reason is that each of the poems is based, in one way or another, on the Hebrew alphabet with its twenty-two consonants. The first, second and third poems are simple acrostics, with each successive verse beginning with the corresponding letter of the alphabet, from Aleph to Tav. The third poem, at the centre of the book, is a more elaborate acrostic. The sixty-six verses are in reality twenty-two verses of three lines each, so that this poem is the same length as the other four. The first three lines begin with Aleph, the second three with Beth, and so on. The final poem is not an acrostic at all, but still conforms to the basic pattern of twenty-two verses.

There is much more to the structure of the book and to the form of the individual poems than this, but three comments are already in order. First, the dominant acrostic patterning is a powerful unifying feature of the book. The five poems are associated by their common structure, which acts as a starting-point for enquiry into their unity at other levels.

Secondly, the variations of form that occur in chapters 3 and 5 tend to draw our attention to these two poems as having a heightened significance within the total composition. This impression is reinforced, in the case of the third poem, by its central location, flanked by two and two. What is to be made of the variation in the fifth poem is less certain. The simpler form compared with the other four may suggest diminished rather than heightened significance. Two considerations count against this, however. This poem stands at the end of the book, and is a communal lament, in contrast to the individual laments which precede it. Given this, the dropping of the strictly acrostic form may represent an 'unravelling', a resolution of some kind, to the issues with which the preceding poems have been struggling. I will argue later that this is in fact the case.

Finally, as Dilbert Hillers (1992: 26–27) has noted, the acrostic form of the poems has the effect of giving grief a shape which is itself a kind of resolution. Grief itself, by its very nature, is a rather formless thing. The mind of a person in deep sorrow characteristically moves in circles, returning again and again to the source of the grief, unable to leave it and unable to resolve it. What the acrostic form does is to allow the grief to be fully expressed, and yet at the same time sets limits to it. These poems explore grief in its many and varied aspects, viewing it first from one perspective, then from another and yet another. The whole gamut of human sorrow is explored; the A to Z of sorrow. And yet, by that same acrostic pattern, the grief is shaped and led to a conclusion, a point of completeness, where everything necessary has been said, at least for the time being, and the mourner can fall silent without feeling he has been stifled. In this sense the acrostic form has more than aesthetic significance; it has therapeutic and pastoral significance as well.

Poem 1: Zion's plight

[1] How deserted lies the city,
    once so full of people!
How like a widow is she,
    who once was great among the nations!
She who was queen among the provinces
    has now become a slave.

This opening verse of chapter 1 establishes a third-person perspective on Zion's plight; the city is viewed initially from the standpoint of an observer. It is not immediately clear, however, whether the observer is friend or foe, and whether the tone is sympathetic or derisive. The opening exclamation, 'How' (*'êkâ*), is ambiguous, and may be taken either way.[2] Furthermore, this ambiguity is dispelled only gradually as the poem unfolds. First a counterpoint is established between third-person and first-person viewpoints, and then the latter takes over and becomes dominant. Hillers (1992: 79) has mapped this psychological progression in the poem as follows:

[2] Cf. 2 Sam. 1:27, 'How ['*êk*] the mighty have fallen!' (a lament), with Is. 14:12, 'How ['*êk*] you have fallen from heaven, O morning star ...!' (a taunt song).

vv. 1–11   The anguish of Zion as seen from without
            (with two brief prayers by Zion herself, in vv. 9c,11c)
vv. 12–22   The anguish of Zion as she herself feels it
            (with two brief recurrences of the previous point of view,
            in vv. 15c, 17)

The tonal ambiguity is resolved as we are led from observation to identification, and see Zion's plight from within, through her own anguished eyes. The poem is structurally sophisticated, but not static; its emotional intensity increases.

The second thing the opening verse does is to introduce a reversal theme, expressed here in the double contrast between greatness[3] and widowhood, 'queen' and 'slave'. This kind of contrast between past glory and present humiliation is typical of ancient funeral songs (cf. Gottwald 1962: ch. 3). It is a theme that will be sustained and reworked in various ways throughout the whole book, and in due course we shall examine some of the variations that are rung upon it. We simply note its presence here, and the fact that it is a major element linking all five poems.

> [2] Bitterly she weeps at night,
>   tears are upon her cheeks.
> Among all her lovers
>   there is none to comfort her.
> All her friends have betrayed her,
>   they have become her enemies.

The picture of Zion weeping bitterly prepares us for the change of perspective to which we have already referred. In the second half of the poem we shall hear Zion's bitter cry directly. Furthermore, the reversal theme is continued here in the contrast between the 'all' and the 'none'. But now it is linked to a second theme expressed in the words, 'there is none to comfort her'. In the following verses this will open out into a refrain that will permeate the entire poem and bind its two halves together:

> [7] When her people fell into enemy hands,
>   there was no-one to help her ...

---

[3] The same term, *rabbātî*, is used of 'great' population and 'great' position in lines 2 and 4 respectively. This is obscured by the NIV.

> [16] 'This is why I weep ...
> No-one is near to comfort me ...'

> [17] Zion stretches out her hands,
> but there is no-one to comfort her.

> [21] 'People have heard my groaning,
> but there is no-one to comfort me.'

This cry finds its definitive answer, of course, in Isaiah 40:1, 'Comfort, comfort my people.'[4] But here there is no hint of such a resolution. Rather, the refrain is the sharp end of a probe that is inserted into the problem to begin to explore its deep-seated causes. Zion has no comforter because all her 'lovers' and 'friends' have deserted her. This is both a statement of fact and an implied accusation. Such lovers and friends were unworthy of Zion's confidence, and she herself has been too quick to run after them. It is a sub-theme hinted at in 1:8 ('Jerusalem ... has become unclean'), and then put with brutal directness in 1:9, 'Her filthiness clung to her skirts; she did not consider her future.' So the refrain ('no-one to comfort her/me') becomes a bridge from the simple depiction of Zion's plight to moral reflection upon it.

But this moral plane of the poem is inherently unstable, because it consists entirely of metaphor. It is not until we break through it and descend to the theological plane that we touch base with the bedrock meaning, for it is here that the issues the poem deals with are spoken of directly. Access to this theological foundation is provided by the explicit references to the LORD (Yahweh), ten all told, which are scattered though the poem:

> [5] ... The LORD has brought her grief,
> because of her many sins.

> [9] ... 'Look, O LORD, on my affliction,
> for the enemy has triumphed.'

> [11] ... 'Look, O LORD, and consider,
> for I am despised.'

---

[4] Moreover, it is specially *Jerusalem's* plight that is on view there (Is. 40:2: 'Speak tenderly to Jerusalem').

[12] ... 'Is any suffering like my suffering ...
that the LORD has brought on me
in the day of his fierce anger?'

[14] 'My sins have been bound into a yoke ...
and the LORD has sapped my strength.
He has handed me over ...'

[15] 'The LORD has rejected
all the warriors in my midst ...
In his winepress the LORD has trampled
the Virgin Daughter of Judah.'

[17] 'The LORD has decreed for Jacob
that his neighbours become his foes.'

[18] 'The LORD is righteous,
yet I rebelled against his command.'

[20] 'See, O LORD, how distressed I am!'

Metaphor is not totally dispensed with at this level,[5] but the categories of thought are now unambiguously theological. The suffering is understood in terms of sin, divine anger, and righteous judgment. The third-person perspective of the first part of the poem and the first-person perspective of the second find their ideological meeting-point here, for the theological understanding of the situation is a shared one. It is first expressed by the observer (1:5), and then accepted by Zion herself (1:18). But it is no easy acceptance we see here. One cannot help but detect a note of protest in Zion's description of her sufferings, and her appeal to others, including Yahweh himself, to see and take note of it. Is there any suffering like her suffering? Has Yahweh ever acted so severely with anyone else? In the context of this struggle, the confession that Yahweh is righteous (1:18) is not arrived at lightly, but only through struggle and deep pain. Here we make contact with an angst which is at the very heart of Israelite religion with its uncompromising monotheism. For if there is but one God, who is sovereign over all things, no final explanation for anything is possible other than that he is behind it, and there is nowhere else to run but into the arms of the very One whose anger you have aroused. This means

[5] E.g. 'yoke', 'winepress', 'Virgin Daughter' (1:14–15).

that, if there is to be any hope of recovery at all, protest must sooner or later give way to repentance and supplication.[6] All these dimensions of a distinctively Israelite response to suffering are encapsulated in this first poem, and worked out more fully in the four which follow.

Poem 2: Yahweh's fierce anger

Our study of the book's structure has drawn attention to poems 3 and 5 as potentially very significant. In order to give these the attention they require, we shall have to treat the other poems in rather more summary fashion.

The principal theme of this second poem (ch. 2) is struck at once by the double reference to Yahweh's anger in the first verse, and is sustained by constant reference to it.[7] This is a poem about Yahweh's fierce and pitiless anger (2:6, 21). It builds on the foundations laid in the first poem, powerfully emphasizing that the destruction of Zion was a deliberate act of Yahweh. The point could scarcely be made more forcibly than in the first eight verses, in which Yahweh is the grammatical subject of every sentence:[8] 'the LORD has covered the Daughter of Zion with the cloud of his anger ... He has hurled down ... he has not remembered ... he has torn down ... he has strung his bow ... He has laid waste ...' and so on. The climax of the first part of the poem is reached in 2:17:

> The LORD has done what he planned,
>   he has fulfilled his word,
>   which he decreed long ago.
> He has overthrown ... without pity.[9]

This conclusion then becomes the basis for an exhortation and response which make up the second half of the poem. There is an inner logic to the whole which might be summarized in the following way:

[6] Cf. the book of Job, with its agonized progress towards Job's repentance in 42:1–6.

[7] His 'anger' (*'ap̄*) is referred to in 2:1, 6, 21, 22; his 'wrath' (*'eḇrâ*) in 2:2; and his acting 'without pity' (*lō' ḥāmal*) in 2:2, 21. The reference to Yahweh as 'an enemy' (*'ōyēḇ*) in 2:5 draws these together in a single, concrete image.

[8] Sometimes the title *'ᵃḏōnāy* ('Lord') is used, as in 2:1, 2, 5, 7, and sometimes the personal name *yhwh* ('Yahweh'), as in 2:8, 9. Significantly it is *yhwh* that is used in the climactic seventeenth verse. Clearly, Yahweh, however he is referred to, is the actual subject in every case.

[9] The NIV adds 'you' after 'overthrown'.

1. It is Yahweh who has destroyed Zion   2:1–17
2. [Therefore] cry out to Yahweh   2:18–19
3. Zion's anguished cry   2:20–22[10]

This second poem dramatizes the monotheistic dilemma which was implicit in the first. At the same time it restates the reversal theme we found there, and heightens it. In terms reminiscent of the dirge for the king of Babylon in Isaiah 14:12–23, Zion's fall is spoken of in cosmic terms. She has been cast down from the heights to the depths, from heaven to earth (2:1), her ruin as vast as the sea (2:13). Generally, this poem returns to the third-person perspective of the first part of poem 1,[11] but again there is an intensification. For now the observer himself is moved to tears, and enters more deeply into Zion's grief (2:11). Observer and observed weep together under the impact of Yahweh's terrible anger (cf. 2:11 with 1:16).

A feature of this poem is the way Zion's ruin is traced, at the human level, to a critical failure of leadership. It is an issue we shall find surfacing strongly again in the fourth poem. King and priest are the special objects of Yahweh's anger in 2:6, though their crimes are not specified. More pointed is the indictment of the prophets in 2:14; their visions were worthless, they did not expose Zion's sin so as to ward off her captivity, and their oracles were false and misleading. It is one of the points in the book where the language is suffused with the spirit of Jeremiah (e.g. Jer. 23:9–40), and we are made aware that behind abstract images lie flesh-and-blood struggles between real people, and between individuals and God. Zion's sin is the sin of her people, and especially of her leaders. It is this awareness, generated by this second poem, which prepares us for the intensely personal nature of the third, central poem of the book.

Poem 3: The man who has seen affliction

Here it is as though the observer of the previous two poems, without ever disclosing his identity, steps forward and gives full vent to his own, personal grief. So *intensely* personal does the language become that for more than half the poem the national dimension of the crisis is lost to view entirely, and all we are aware of is this man's pain and his

---

[10] Cf. Hillers 1992: 103.

[11] Zion herself speaks only in the last three verses (2:20–22). The first-person voice of 2:11, and 13, is that of an observer, not of Zion herself. This is particularly clear in 2:13, 'What can I say for you … ?'

struggle to come to terms with it. 'I am the man' (3:1). For a time it is as though there is no other. He has become absorbed in his own struggles and, by default, has handed the role of observer over to us.

This poem is far more complex than the previous two, and does not yield so easily to formal analysis. The main structural feature (apart from the acrostic) is the way the question of verse 39, 'Why should a living man complain, a man (*geber*) for the punishment of his sins?' (my translation), echoes the opening line of the poem, 'I am the man (*haggeber*) who has seen affliction', and effectively closes the first major movement. It marks a significant point of transition in this particular man's journey through his own pain, and his re-engagement with the pain of others. We shall reflect more on this in a moment, but first we need to note how this point is arrived at. The main carriers of the central thematic development in 3:1–39 are the roots *yhl* and *qwh* and their cognates. They both carry the basic meaning 'to wait expectantly', 'to hope'.

[18] So I say, 'My splendour is gone
and all that I had hoped for [*yhl*] from the LORD.'
[21] Yet this I call to mind
and therefore I have hope [*yhl*]
[24] '... the LORD is my portion;
therefore I will wait for [*yhl*] him.
[25] The LORD is good to those whose hope [*qwh*] is in him ...
[29] Let him bury his face in the dust –
there may yet be hope [*qwh*].

We might call 3:1–18 'the eclipse of hope'. It is a personal lament with striking similarities to the corresponding part of the previous poem. Here again Yahweh is the subject of every, or in this case nearly every, sentence. But as if to symbolize the painful estrangement that is felt, the man refers to Yahweh as 'he' rather than by name: 'He has driven me away ... he has turned his hand against me ... he has broken my bones ... he has walled me in ... dragged me from the path ... mangled me ... pierced my heart ... broken my teeth ... trampled me in the dust' (3:1–16). The language is violent and the emotion intense. The man feels like an animal, harried and hunted down by a merciless adversary intent on his total destruction. Only at the very end, when his emotion his spent itself, and his mood becomes more wistful and reflective, does he dare to name his foe directly, and even then with circumspection, as if only too aware of the danger of blasphemy:

> [17] I have been deprived of peace;
>> I have forgotten what prosperity is.
> [18] So I say,
>> My splendour gone
>> And my hope (*yhl*) from Yahweh (my translation).

Here the reversal theme which we found in the first two poems is crystallized in the experience of a single individual. He is a man who once knew 'peace', 'prosperity', and 'splendour', but now knows only the loss of all of them (cf. Gottwald 1962: 59). Yahweh, who had been the source of his hope, has become its destroyer.

But here we are on the threshold of a paradox which lies at the very heart of this central poem. For it is precisely at this point, where hope is extinguished, that, phoenix-like, it begins to rise again. This is a different kind of reversal: a reversal which is internal rather than external, psychological rather than material. It happens as one kind of remembering gives place to another:

> [19] I remember my affliction and my wandering,
>> the bitterness and the gall.
> [20] I well remember them,
>> and my soul is downcast within me.
> [21] Yet this I call to mind
>> and therefore I have hope [*yhl*].

The 'remembering' of 3:19–20 is involuntary, determined by circumstance. The 'calling to mind' of 3:21, however, is deliberate; a choice the sufferer has made. It is in this choice that hope is reborn.

But at the same time it is clear that something more is involved than a determined change to a more positive frame of mind, as though hope had been conjured up out of thin air by a sheer act of the will. The substance for it resides not so much in the choice itself as in what has been chosen: 'Yet *this* I call to mind, and *therefore* I have hope.' The content of the hope is given in the confession which immediately follows in 3:22–23:

> [22] Because of the LORD's great love we are not consumed,
>> For his compassions never fail.
> [23] They are new every morning;
>> great is your faithfulness.

Hope is reborn with the realization that even to be *able* to lament is a gift. For to weep is to be alive, and to that extent, at least, an object of divine grace: 'Because of the LORD's great love we are not consumed.' And with that, the great covenant words that had always defined God rise to the sufferer's mind again in quick succession: 'great love' (*ḥeseḏ*), 'compassion' (*raḥam*), 'faithfulness' (*'ᵉmûnâ*). They or their cognates are all found together in the great covenantal confession of Exodus 34:6:

> The LORD, the LORD, the compassionate [*raḥûm*] and gracious God, slow to anger, abounding in love [*ḥeseḏ*] and faithfulness ['*emeṭ*] ...

This was the confession that distilled the essence of the deeper knowledge of God that had come out of the pain of the golden-calf incident. Yahweh's anger was real, but not hasty or irrational, and it did not nullify the essential truth about him which had been revealed in the exodus. Judgment was part of the covenant relationship, but did not bring it to an end. The continuance of the relationship was guaranteed by the compassion, love and faithfulness of God on which it was founded.[12]

This is the truth about Yahweh that the man calls to mind, and in doing so finds that it is still true. The joy of the discovery is conveyed by the beauty and freshness with which it is expressed. The ancient creed is not simply repeated. Rather, its essence is grasped and given new life in poetry which is uniquely this man's own. He has not merely remembered it, but has appropriated it afresh amid the pain of his present crisis. And what he has done, he has done not only for himself but for others. For his confession is inclusive. It binds him to others and them to him in a *community* which may dare to hope again. 'Because of the LORD's great love *we* are not consumed.' It is the beginning, not only of his recovery, but of theirs as well.

However, he is not quite ready yet to engage his fellows directly. That will come in the second half of the poem. What follows immediately, in 3:24–39, is best understood as a kind of meditation by the man on his experience to this point – a careful turning it over in his

---

[12] Cf. Peterson (1992: 135): 'Again and again we are told [in the OT] that God's love or kindness (*ḥeseḏ*) goes on forever (Jer. 33:11; Pss. 100:5; 106:1; 107:1; 118:1–4; 135:1–26; Ezra 3:11). We are never told that his anger goes on forever.' Eternal punishment is a reality in the OT (e.g. Is. 66:24), but the emphasis clearly falls on Yahweh's persevering commitment to those he has called into covenant relationship with himself.

mind in order to grasp its full significance. And in keeping with the inclusiveness of the language he has already used, he sees his own experience as typical, a particular instance of what is good for all in such circumstances to do:

> ²⁴ I say to myself, 'The LORD is *my* portion;
> therefore I will wait for him.'
> ²⁵ The LORD is good to *those* whose hope is in him,
> to *the one* who seeks him;
> ²⁶ It is good to wait quietly
> for the salvation of the LORD.
> ²⁷ It is good for *a man* [*geḇer*] to bear the yoke
> while he is young (my italics).

Weeping has subsided, and the poem has moved into the reflective style of psalmic wisdom, especially Psalm 34 (which is also an acrostic), where we have exactly the same movement from personal experience to generalization:

> ⁴ *I* sought the LORD, and he answered *me*;
> he delivered *me* from all *my* fears.
> ⁵ *Those* who look to him are radiant;
> *their* faces are never covered with shame.
> (my italics)

In other words, the sufferer of Lamentations 3 is beginning to assume the posture of a sage, and with the occurrence of the key word 'man' (*geḇer*) in verse 27, we are already on the way to the climax in verse 39, where he will cross the threshold from reflection to direct exhortation. But there is one more issue that must surface and be squarely faced first: the delicate and painful matter of sin, personal sin; the recognition that, for all the horror of it, his suffering has been deserved.

> Why should a living man (*'āḏām*) complain,
> a man (*geḇer*) for the punishment of *his sins*?
> (my translation)

There *is* such a thing as undeserved suffering, as the book of Job clearly recognizes. But this man is no Job, and the community of which he is a part is not a blameless one, as the previous poems have made

70

clear. And in such circumstances even lament can be a strategy of evasion. Only when it includes confession of sin does it fully come to grips with reality and allow the love, compassion and faithfulness of God to heal what is broken and make restoration complete. Lament without confession is merely complaint. It is with the recognition of this that the man's personal journey is complete and he is ready to address his fellows and take them with him along the same road.

So 3:39 is both a point of arrival and a point of departure. It is the transition into the second part of the poem in which the man no longer weeps alone, but weeps as part of the community, for no single person's sin produced the sufferings that followed Jerusalem's fall, and no single person should mourn for them alone (cf. Peterson 1992: 142). Hence the exhortation with which the second part of the poem opens:

> [40] Let *us* examine *our* ways and test them,
> and let *us* return to the LORD.
> [41] Let *us* lift up *our* hearts and *our* hands
> to God in heaven, and say:
> [42] '*We* have sinned and rebelled
> and you have not forgiven' (my italics).

It is an exhortation the man can now deliver with complete integrity.

The second part of the poem now develops in a similar way to the first: a lament culminates in an expression of despair (3:43–54), but then hope returns (as indicated by the calling on God in 3:54), and from there on the mood is one of confidence. There is a mixture of third-person and first-person speech forms, but that is not to be wondered at in view of the relationship between individual and community that the earlier part of the poem has forged. The man no longer speaks for himself alone, but for all his fellows. Zion is his city; its people are his people (3:51), and their enemies (3:46) are his also (3:62). He has become both an exhorter and an intercessor. He sees Yahweh as no longer *against* him but *for* him, and as the one who will finally vindicate both him and his fellows against their common foes (3:64–66). The anger that has been vented on them will in time be turned against their enemies. For there is more sin to be dealt with than their own, and the man is confident that God will not rest until *all* wrongs have been righted. What he has laboured to do is to engender that same confidence in the community as a whole. Whether he has been successful is uncertain at this stage. We are left to await clarification in what follows.

Poem 4: Zion's death throes

As foreshadowed, we must treat this poem more briefly. It occupies a position in the book's overall design analogous to that of poem 2, and has a number of affinities with it. After the complexity and intensity of poem 3, there is a reversion here to a simpler acrostic pattern,[13] and a predominantly third-person perspective. What is described is just as horrific as in the previous poem – perhaps even more so; but the tone is more detached and impersonal. Only in 4:17–20 does the poet make explicit his direct involvement with the events by speaking in the first-person plural. The first-person singular is not used at all.

There are two basic parts. The first, in 4:1–20, describes the suffering of the city's inhabitants, especially during the siege, climaxing in the fall of the city and the flight and capture of the king (4:17–20). The second is much briefer, consisting solely of a curse on Edom and a blessing on Zion (4:21–22). The worst is past for Zion, but not for Edom, who will surely be judged for gloating over Zion's downfall.

This poem's special contribution to the book is seen most clearly in the particular way it depicts the suffering of Zion and identifies its cause. It impresses on us the comprehensive nature of the tragedy by showing how every segment of the city's population was affected by it (cf. Gottwald 1962: 59). Young men, the 'precious sons of Zion' (4:2), infants (4:4), the pampered upper classes (4:5), the nobility (4:7–8), nursing mothers (4:10), prophets and priests (4:13–15), even the king himself (4:20) – none escaped. The suffering was intense, and agonizingly prolonged. In this sense it was worse even than that of Sodom (4:6). And the most tragic thing of all is that it could have been avoided: 'it happened because of the sins of her prophets and the iniquities of her priests' (4:13). This poem agrees with poem 2 in tracing Zion's fall to a failure of the nation's religious leaders, especially the prophets. In 2:14 they failed to expose the nation's sin. Here in 4:13, together with the priests, they themselves are said to have been actively involved in that sin, especially violence and oppression of the righteous. Interestingly, the failure of the supreme leader, the king, is dealt is dealt with far more circumspectly. This, we may presume, is partly due to the poet's respect for his office. The king is referred to with extreme deference in 4:20 as 'The LORD's anointed ... under whose shadow we thought that we would live among the nations' (my translation). But the circumspection is also due, almost certainly, to the

---

[13] And with only two lines per stanza instead of three.

poet's own former involvement in, and endorsement of, the king's policies, as suggested by 4:17:

> Moreover, our eyes failed,
>> looking in vain for help;
> from our towers we watched
>> for a nation that could not save us.

The king and those associated with him had presided over a political policy that had proved useless in Zion's hour of desperate need. We are left to wonder about any complicity of the court in the sins of the priests and prophets. It is a matter about which this poet has chosen to remain silent (in stark contrast to Jeremiah). What none of the leaders did was to call for repentance and a wholehearted return to dependence on Yahweh.

Poem 5: The community at prayer

We have already noted in a preliminary way how our attention is drawn to this poem both by its place in the book's structure and by its distinctive form. It is the last poem. If our passage through the book may be likened to a journey, this is the point of arrival. And this poem is markedly different from the others in a number of ways. Only an echo of the acrostic pattern remains in the twenty-two-verse format. It is shorter than the other poems, each verse having only one line. And the circumstances depicted in it suggest a situation in which, while the effects of the disaster are still strongly felt, the event itself is now some time past. Zion lies desolate, 'with jackals prowling over it' (5:18). The remaining population struggles to survive in the surrounding countryside and the ruined towns. But even there they find themselves at the mercy of foreigners who have seized whatever of value remained (5:2–3). They are constantly harried by enemies; they have to work as virtual slaves (5:13), buy water to drink (5:4), and search for food at the risk of their lives (5:9). We are back to the basic situation depicted in poem 1,[14] but now the grim particulars are given more fully. The aftermath is almost as difficult to endure as the disaster itself.

This final poem is in the first-person plural throughout, and is a more or less straightforward example of a communal lament (cf. e.g. Pss. 44; 80). The scattered community has gathered, possibly at the temple site

---

[14] Especially 1:1, 'How deserted lies the city ...!' Other links with ch. 1 include the references to 'no rest' in 5:5 (cf. 1:3), and to the 'days as of old' in 5:21 (cf. 1:7).

in the ruined city itself. What has drawn them together is a common
determination to lay their whole situation before Yahweh and appeal to
him for help. In other words, what their leaders had failed to do for
them (to call them back to wholehearted dependence on God), the bitter
experience of Yahweh's anger has done. As Eugene Peterson (1992:
132) has observed, 'prayer is suffering's best result', and that is exactly
what we find here. This poem is a prayer from beginning to end. It
moves from an initial call to Yahweh to listen (5:1), to a final appeal to
him for help (5:20–21). In between, there is a long description of the
plight of the community (5:2–18), and a brief, hymn-like confession of
Yahweh's sovereignty (5:19). All these are normal features of a
communal lament.

Three features, however, require special comment. They all relate in
one way or another to the special relationship between this final poem
and the central third poem. The first is the strong note of repentance
that is present. At first it seems as though the mourners see themselves
as the innocent victims of others' sins: 'Our fathers sinned and are no
more, and we bear their punishment' (5:7). But verse 16 shows that this
is merely a step on the way to something more profound, for there it is
their *own* sin that they confess: 'The crown has fallen from our head.
Woe to us, for *we* have sinned!' (my italics). They lament the fact that
the long-threatened judgment has fallen upon their own generation, but
acknowledge that they are just as sinful as their fathers. Repentance is
also evident in the appeal at the end of the poem: 'Restore us to
yourself, O LORD ...' (5:21). Rightly understood, this is an appeal for
forgiveness and restored relationship rather than simply for a change of
circumstances. This poem is more than a lament; it is a prayer of
penitence. It shows the community following the lead given them by
'the man' of chapter 3.

The second noteworthy feature is the confession of faith in 5:19:

> You, O LORD, reign for ever;
> your throne endures from generation to generation.

This corresponds formally to the positive confession of the man in
poem 3; and it is a turning here as his was there. But in content the two
confessions are strikingly different. The man's confession was of
Yahweh's great love, his compassion and his faithfulness (3:22–23).
This speaks simply of his enduring sovereignty, his 'throne' (*kissē'*).
The outcome, if there is to be one, will be determined by Yahweh. That
is all. The one possible hint of something more is in the expression

'from generation to generation', picking up the earlier reference to this generation's solidarity with their fathers. If sin extends from generation to generation, and so does judgment, may not mercy as well? It is a slender confidence, barely discernible. But at least it is enough to keep the prayer going a little longer. The confession of 5:19 is in fact a bridge into the final appeal, which closes both this poem and the book as a whole.

The plaintive, questioning ending of this poem is very far from the boldness with which the third poem ended. There is no mention of enemies being paid back; the entire focus is on how Yahweh will respond to the mourners themselves. Even their repentance will be unavailing unless Yahweh reaches over the gap that separates them from him and draws them across: 'Restore us to yourself, [Yahweh], *that we may return*' (5:21, my italics). And even this is framed by questions that reveal just how racked with doubt the community still is. Why does Yahweh forget them? Why forsake them for so long? Has he utterly rejected them? The last attribute of God to be mentioned is not his mercy, but his anger (5:22). This is a prayer of desperate people who have been convinced of their sinfulness and know they have nowhere else to go but to Yahweh, but remain uncertain about how he will receive them. They have followed the lead of the man of chapter 3 as far as they are able, but lack his bold faith. And so the book ends with a question rather than an answer. Only the future, it seems will reveal whether or not the man's confidence in the unfailing nature of Yahweh's mercy has been justified.

II

There are two ancient traditions about where Lamentations most appropriately belongs in the Old Testament canon. The first, reflected in the LXX and Josephus, locates it in the Prophets, immediately after Jeremiah, partly at least because it was attributed to him as its author. There are considerable difficulties with this view of its authorship. We have already encountered one of them in passing in chapter 4, where the the poet's stance towards the king is in stark contrast to that of Jeremiah. What is more deeply embedded in this tradition, however, is the recognition that the book is prophetic in character; that it wrestles, as the prophets did, with the question of how God was at work in Israel's history, and especially in one critical episode of it.

The second tradition, reflected in the Talmud, places Lamentations

among the Writings. Its earliest location here, apparently on chronological grounds, was towards the end of the Writings, just before
Daniel and Esther (cf. Hillers 1992: 7). From the early medieval
period, however, it has been placed among the Five Scrolls, at the
centre of the Writings. This is related to its liturgical use on the Ninth
of Ab.[15] Common to both these traditions is the awareness that
Lamentations is rooted in history. It is not about suffering in general,
but the suffering associated with a particular, critical moment in
Yahweh's administration of his covenant relationship with Israel. This
is its first and most obvious relationship to its Old Testament context.

The second is the way it interacts with specific Old Testament
traditions that relate, in one way or another, to the theological
significance of this critical moment in Israel's history. The major
contributions to discussion of this important issue have been those of
Gottwald in the 1950s and Albrektson in the 1960s.[16] Gottwald drew
attention to the many echoes in Lamentations of the covenant curses of
Deuteronomy 28.[17] With this in mind, and taking into account the note
of protest which frequently surfaces in the book, Gottwald argued that
the theological issue that lay at the heart of Lamentations was a
perceived disjunction between deuteronomic theology and historical
reality. Deuteronomic theology had posited a correspondence between
obedience and blessing. But the reforms of Josiah, the most thorough-
going recall to covenant faithfulness in Israel's history, had been
followed in quick succession by the violent death of the reformer
himself, and a rapid deterioration in the nation's fortunes culminating
in the fall of Jerusalem. The fall of Jerusalem appeared to make
nonsense of deuteronomic theology and plunged Israel into a
theological crisis.

That such may in fact have happened is a plausible enough suggestion
that warrants further critical reflection.[18] But Gottwald's thesis can
hardly stand as a reading of Lamentations. Allusions to Deuteronomy

---

[15] The fifth month of the Jewish religious calendar, corresponding roughly to July-
August. According to Jewish tradition, the second temple fell to the Romans under Titus
on the Ninth of Ab.

[16] Gottwald 1962, first published in 1954; Albrektson 1963.

[17] E.g. Lam. 1:3, 5, 9; 2:20, 3:45; 4:10, 16; 5:12.

[18] That the exile plunged Israel into a theological crisis is hardly open to question.
However, if that crisis had any connection at all with deuteronomic theology, it may
have had more to do with a *misunderstanding* of it rather than with any actual clash
between it and historical reality. Barker (1998) has argued persuasively that
Deuteronomy in fact anticipates Israel's failure and locates hope for the future in
Yahweh's grace and faithfulness rather than in Israel's obedience. Cf. Sailhamer 1991;
Dempster 1997.

certainly exist, and deuteronomic theology must be acknowledged as a significant contributor to Lamentations. But the fact is that such theology is never once called into question in this scroll. On the contrary, Jerusalem's sin and Yahweh's righteousness in judging her are both fully acknowledged. Deuteronomic theology, which included curse as well as blessing, is not a *problem* in Lamentations, but a *frame of reference* which allows the tragedy to be understood:

> The LORD has done what he planned;
> he has fulfilled his word,
> which he decreed long ago (2:17).

In this respect the theology of Lamentations is closely aligned with that of 2 Kings, which regards Judah's apostasy as so persistent and grave that even Josiah's reforms could not avert Yahweh's wrath (23: 26–27). This is not to deny that there is an element of protest in Lamentations, but the reason for it must be sought elsewhere.

Albrektson was on much firmer ground when he located the theological angst of the book in the area of Zion theology, especially as expressed in liturgical pieces such as Psalms 46, 48 and 76. Specific allusions are fewer than to Deuteronomy, occurring mainly in chapters 2 and 4,[19] but they are transparent and unmistakable.[20] Such links make it clear that the reversal theme we found recurring in the poems must be seen in relation to the theology espoused in such psalms. And here indeed lies a clash between theology and history, for these psalms had proclaimed the election of Zion, and therefore her impregnability, in apparently absolute terms.[21] The shock-waves of this clash reverberate through the whole book. Zion theology, like the Richter scale, identifies the shattering dimensions of the disaster, but provides no way of explaining it. Recourse must be had to the Sinai covenant, with its 'blessing and curse' theology, before explanation becomes possible.

But of course that is a solution which leaves Zion theology stranded. What is to be done with it in the light of 587 BC? Must it simply be given up as discredited, or does it encapsulate some truth that may survive? It is no mean question, for at heart Zion theology is about the

---

[19] Lam. 2:15 (cf. Pss. 48:3; 50:2); 4:12 (cf. Ps. 76:13); 4:20 (cf. Ps. 2); 5:20 (cf. Pss. 46:5; 48:2).

[20] Cf. e.g. Lam. 2:15, 'Is this the city that was called the perfection of beauty, the joy of the whole earth?', with Ps. 48:2, 'beautiful in its loftiness, the joy of the whole earth', and Ps. 50:2, 'Out of Zion, the perfection of beauty, God shines forth' (my translation).

[21] E.g. Ps. 46:5, 7: 'God is within her, she will not fall; God will help her at break of day ... The LORD Almighty is with us; the God of Jacob is our fortress.'

election of Israel: David as the chosen king, Jerusalem and the temple as the chosen place and (by extension) Israel as the chosen nation. Does 587 BC mean that the doctrine of election, and hence the whole covenant relationship between Yahweh and Israel, is at an end? This is the question that hangs in the air as the book comes to a close. Lamentations as such provides no definitive answer to it, though the confession of the man in chapter 3 suggests one. Dumbrell has put his finger on the issue in a way that shows an acute awareness of the larger theological context in which Lamentations must be viewed. What have been lost are the externals of election; the outward signs of it. Reliance on these brought Israel to ruin. But 'the election of Israel preceded all externals. Yahweh, who had selected her, would continue with her if he chose' (Dumbrell 1988: 251). It might yet be possible to speak truly of an impregnable city of God, but how remains to be seen.

Two final comments are called for about the relationship of Lamentations to its Old Testament context. First, while deuteronomic theology and Zion theology may be keys, they are not all there is to the theology of Lamentations. As we have seen, the five poems draw not only on Deuteronomy 28 and the Zion psalms, but on the lament, penitential, and imprecatory psalms, on the credal confession of Exodus 34 and its echoes elsewhere in the Torah, and on the content and forms of wisdom discourse about suffering and the proper response to it. Lamentations is in fact linked to its Old Testament context at many levels. It draws on all the theological resources at its disposal and focuses them on the problem at hand. It is a parade example of applied theology.

Finally, though, it must be remembered that Lamentations is about a tragedy that was intensely human. The five poems are as much about the *experience* of suffering as about its causes, and the element of protest running through them shows a struggle between heart and head, between theological acceptance and moral outrage:

> 'Look, O LORD, and consider ...
> Should women eat their offspring,
>   the children they have cared for?' (2:20).

At one level the divine anger is acknowledged to be right. But at another it remains simply unendurable. It cannot be borne with equanimity, however much that may be an ideal to which to aspire. When all available theological resources have been called upon, the fact remains that the anger of God and the suffering it produces are overwhelmingly shocking realities from which only God himself can give relief. The book of Lamentations, more than any other Old Testament book, shows us God's wrath as a directly experienced reality.

III

Our final task is to ask what significance the book of Lamentations takes on when it is viewed in the light of the fuller revelation we have in the New Testament. Fundamental to this is the need to bear clearly in mind exactly what kind of book it is and the nature of the questions with which it leaves us.

First, it is a book about suffering, but not suffering in general. It is about deserved suffering, suffering for sin. And it is about the suffering of the people of God, suffering within the covenant, so to speak. Secondly, it is a book about repentance; a study in godly sorrow, the sorrow that leads to repentance (cf. 2 Cor. 7:8–11). Finally, it is a book that leaves us with questions. What will become of Israel's election? Will God forgive his people when they repent, or not? Will he be compassionate, or will he utterly reject them? It is a book that presses us to the brink of the failure of the old covenant through the sinfulness of the people of God. The issue for us here is: what happens beyond Lamentations, so to speak? Is it simply left behind, or are the issues it raises taken up and brought to a point of resolution of some kind? It would be interesting to see what lines of development might be traced in the post-exilic and intertestamental literature. But constraints of space and the terms of reference I have set myself require me, for the remainder of this chapter, to focus specifically on the New Testament.

An initial difficulty is the fact that there are no quotations from Lamentations in the New Testament. This leaves us without specific instances of how the New Testament writers saw it to be relevant to the gospel, and even raises the possibility that they did not see it to be relevant at all. There do appear to be *allusions* to it, however.[22] In pronouncing judgment on Simon the sorcerer in Acts 8:23, Peter declares that he (Simon) is 'in the gall of bitterness and in the bond of iniquity' (RSV), an expression paralleled in the Septuagint version of Lamentations 3:15. Paul's striking statement in 1 Corinthians 4:13, 'we have become ... as the refuse of the world, the offscouring of all

---

[22] Those I refer to in the following section are listed in the index of allusions and verbal parallels in Aland et al. (eds.) 1983: 908.

things', closely reflects Lamentations 3:45. The context is the willingness of Paul and his fellow-apostles to suffer like condemned men as part of their identification with Christ. And the references to the winepress of God's wrath being trodden outside the city in Revelation 14:20 and 19:15 recall Lamentations 1:15, where it is trodden in Jerusalem itself.[23] It is as though Lamentations has gone down into the subconscious of the New Testament writers and produces echoes at times, especially when judgment is on view.

Of particular interest is a probable allusion to Lamentations in Mark's account of the crucifixion. In Lamentations 2:15, at the height of Zion's suffering, those who pass by scoff at her, shaking their heads and saying, 'Is this the city that was called the perfection of beauty?' In Mark 15:29–30, when Jesus is in his final agony on the cross, those who pass by hurl insults at him, shaking their heads and saying, 'You who are going to destroy the temple and build it in three days, come down from the cross ...!' The similarities are striking, and the matching contexts in which they occur highly suggestive. Taking his cue from this, Kenneth Bailey (1991) has argued that Mark 15:20–39 is a tightly constructed rhetorical unit, beginning with a Jewish proselyte, Simon of Cyrene, carrying Jesus' cross, and ending with a Roman centurion confessing that he was truly the Son of God. The unit consists of ten elements, symmetrically arranged in five matching pairs, with the abuse of Jesus by the passers-by and the chief priests falling at the very centre. The mockery pointedly draws attention to the connection between the destruction of the temple and the crucifixion of Jesus. Bailey argues that Mark wrote his account of the cross in the shadow of the fall of Jerusalem in AD 70, and drew on language originally used to describe the earlier fall of the city in 587 BC. But he adapted it in line with his rhetorical purpose.

> He shifts the focus from the *city* to the *person* and expands the story to include mockery *and faith*. The passion story now describes a holy of holies permanently revealed and a new temple destined to be rebuilt in three days through resurrection (1991: 105).

In short, Christ crucified is the God-given replacement for Jerusalem and the temple.

Echoes and allusions, by their very nature, are difficult to identify with certainty, and Bailey's thesis is open to question at certain

---

[23] What happened inside the city will one day happen outside it, in the world at large.

points.[24] At the very least, however, the probable allusions to Lamentations that we have mentioned should be seen as straws in the wind, and what they suggest is confirmed by the structure of New Testament theology as a whole. The questions Lamentations posed so acutely are not left behind, but brought to definitive resolution in the New Testament gospel. The broader canonical context enables us to move beyond the tentative note on which Lamentations ends. The unfailing love and righteous wrath of which it speaks find their climactic meeting-point in the cross.[25] The wrath of God as an awful reality to be reckoned with is not nullified, but reserved only for those who refuse what the cross offers them.[26] The election of Israel is not so much brought to an end as fulfilled in the creation of a new people of God, open to all who, like the centurion, confess Jesus as the Son of God.[27] It is in the light of this resolution that the New Testament is able to speak with fresh certainty of forgiveness for those who repent,[28] and of a city of God which can never be destroyed, the home of the redeemed for ever.[29]

The special contribution of Lamentations is to confront us with the terrible reality of the wrath of God, and so bars the way to any resolution less than the one the New Testament finally provides.[30] It is a dark and heavy garment, but with gold worked into it; a penitential robe, terrible and glorious. It is a garment for sinners to wear as they make their way, trembling yet hopeful, to the cross of Christ.

---

[24] The historical elements of his argument (e.g. the circumstances in which Mark wrote his Gospel) are in principle incidental to the rhetorical elements (the structure and theology of Mark 15:20–39). The central issue is whether the allusion in question is to Lam. 2:15–16 or to Ps. 22:7. There is certainly a quotation from Ps. 22:1 in the immediate context. But there is also an allusion to the the Elijah prophecy of Mal. 4:5–6. In other words, there are connections with a number of OT texts. Bailey has made a strong case, in my judgment, that the most extensive parallels in the key central verses of the passage (Mark 15:29–30) are with Lam. 2:15–16. Also, the reference to the destruction of the temple in the abuse hurled at Jesus strongly suggests a connection with Lamentations.

[25] Eph. 2:3–7; Rom. 5:6–9; 1 Thess. 1:10.

[26] Rom. 2:8; 2 Thess. 1:5–10.

[27] Rom. 9:1–5; 11:1–24.

[28] Luke 24:45–47; 1 John 1:8–9.

[29] Rev. 21:1 – 22:5.

[30] While this solution is *anticipated* in the many displays of God's grace in the OT, it is *found* only in the cross of Christ.

Chapter Four

Ecclesiastes
Garment of vexation

Now we see through a glass, darkly.
1 Corinthians 13:12, AV

Ecclesiastes is perhaps the most enigmatic book in the Old Testament. Like the desert Sphinx, it teases us with questions, yields its secrets only grudgingly, and will not allow us the luxury of easy answers. In other words, it is thoroughly irritating, but at the same time almost mesmeric in its appeal. It draws us towards it by mirroring the perplexity we all feel as we grapple with life.

Our ultimate goal is to understand how Ecclesiastes relates to the New Testament gospel, but where shall we start? There are virtually no assured results of scholarly study to provide a foothold for us. Ecclesiastes has effectively scattered the academic field rather than drawing it together around any widely held conclusions. The only point on which there is anything approaching consensus is that it is a relatively late work, in which the kind of confident wisdom associated with Solomon is viewed rather critically in the light of radically changed circumstances. This may well be correct, and merits careful consideration in so far as it is relevant to our purpose. But, given the specific terms of reference I have set myself, our starting-point must be the book of Ecclesiastes itself. Only when we have heard its own distinct voice, as best we can, shall we be able to evaluate how it interacts with other voices.

I

We begin with a consideration of how Ecclesiastes is structured: how it begins and ends, what distinct parts are discernible, and how they appear to be related to one another. This should give us at least a provisional orientation to it, and some clues as to how it works as a literary composition. Furthermore, since we are not able to examine the entire book in detail here, some sense of its overall design is necessary to guide us in selecting passages, or key expressions, to scrutinize more closely.

At once we meet a difficulty, however. For structure is one of the most vexed issues in the study of Ecclesiastes. At the end of the nineteenth century, Franz Delitzsch, frustrated with his own attempts to delineate its structure, predicted that all future attempts would also fail. And so far he has been proved right, at least in the sense that no thorough-going analysis of the main body of the book has been able to command wide assent. Nevertheless, real advances have been made in recent years, and at least some basic elements of design are now generally recognized.

Voices and frames

For the moment we shall adopt the NIV's rendering of key expressions such as *qōhelet* ('the Teacher') and *h*ᵉ*bēl h*ᵉ*bālîm* ('Meaningless! Meaningless!'), reserving closer examination of them till later.

Two voices address us in Ecclesiastes. In the main body of the work we hear the Teacher speaking in the first person and addressing us directly: 'I, the Teacher, was king over Israel in Jerusalem' (1:12), 'I thought in my heart' (2:1), 'I have seen another evil under the sun' (6:1), 'So I reflected on all this' (9:1), and so on. But the book begins and ends with another voice that introduces the Teacher to us, and speaks about him in the third person: 'The words of the Teacher, son of David, king of Jerusalem' (1:1), and in the epilogue, 'Not only was the Teacher wise, but also he imparted knowledge to the people' (12:9). There is one brief occurrence of this second voice in the body of the book at 7:27: '"Look," says the Teacher, "this is what I have discovered."' Michael Fox (1977) in particular has drawn attention to the key importance of this second voice. The words of the Teacher are framed and interpreted for us by the voice of this 'frame narrator', who is the author of the book. In order to hear what the book has to say, we shall need to be attuned to both voices, but the second is the interpreter of the first. It is in the epilogue of 12:9–14 that this voice speaks most expansively.

We can take this further, however. If the frame narrator is the author of the book, we may expect his interpretive influence to be felt in other, more subtle ways as well, such as the manner in which the material of the book is configured. While it may be difficult to describe this in detail, there is certainly more to the design of the book than the presence of a superscription and an epilogue. After the superscription comes the key thematic statement, 'Meaningless! Meaningless! ... Everything is meaningless' (1:2), which is repeated in 12:8, immediately before the epilogue. If we move further inwards, we find an introductory poem in 1:4–11, and a closing poem in 12:1–7.[1] Both have to do with the impermanent, fleeting nature of human existence. In the first, the generations come and go like the endlessly repeating patterns of the sun, wind and rivers. Nothing of lasting significance is achieved. In the second, the underlying cause of this impermanence and futility is contemplated directly: death eventually claims every person, and therefore every generation. And closer examination reveals further links between these two poems.[2]

We would seem to be justified, therefore, in extending the notion of 'frame' from voices to broader structural features. The body of the book is framed by a superscription, a thematic statement and an opening poem at the beginning, and three corresponding elements in reverse order at the end: closing poem, same thematic statement, epilogue.

The design of the book as a whole

The task of identifying the structure becomes much more difficult when we move from the outer frame to the material that falls within it. The 1960s and 1970s, in particular, saw a number of determined efforts to crack the code of the book's basic design. Ginsberg (1960) focused on what he saw to be major movements of thought, and identified four sections in an ABAB pattern. Castellino (1968), noting the abrupt change to the imperative at 5:1 (MT 4:17), divided the book into two halves at that point. Wright (1976), paying more attention to patterns of verbal repetition and corresponding repetition of ideas, found the significant division to be after 6:9, on the grounds that this is the last occurrence of the statement that all is vanity and a chasing after wind. Kaiser (1979) took the positive refrain, 'eat and drink and find satisfaction in ... work' (2:24; cf. 3:13; 5:18; 8:15), as a concluding

---

[1] Or possibly 11:9 – 12:7.

[2] E.g. *šemeš* ('sun') and *rûaḥ* ('wind, spirit') are common to the two. In the first, *rûaḥ* is used of the wind that returns endlessly on its circuits. In the second it is used of the human breath or spirit that returns to God at death. The verb *zkr* ('to remember') and its cognate noun *zikrôn* ('remembrance') are another important link. In the opening poem there is 'no remembrance' of former generations by those who come after them. The closing poem enjoins each individual, in each one's fleeting lifetime, to 'remember' his or her Creator.

marker, and divided the material into four parts, the fourth opening out into the more expansive positive teaching with which the book ends. And this is merely a brief sampling of the kind of work that his been done and continues to be done.

The disagreements illustrate the difficulty of the task. Positively, they show that there are many potential indicators of structure: verbal repetitions, changes of style, movements of thought, and so on. In principle, the most adequate analysis will be one that is able to show the greatest degree of alignment between the various indicators. By this standard, Wright's is the most impressive of those we have just surveyed. But it runs into difficulties with its division of the book at 6:9. The theme he assigns to the second half of the book (human inability to find out / know the work of God) is also prominent in the first half (especially in 3:11, 21–22; cf. also 2:19: 5:1). The artificiality of this division is symptomatic of a passion for neatness, a rigidity which does not sufficiently recognize the complexity of the material.

It is not possible for me here to offer a complete analysis of my own. Happily, however, a study by Stephen de Jong (1992) incorporates some of the best insights of previous work without falling into the kind of rigidity which has marred it. It seems to me to represent precisely the kind of judicious analysis that is called for. De Jong's analysis is guided by what he calls three 'intuitions':

> The first is that we have to start with stylistic and semantic observations. The second is that the structure of the book can only be described adequately if we reckon not only with one structuring principle, but with more. The third intuition is that in structuring the book the writer did not apply modern Western standards, such as absolute consistency and systematism. We have to look for principles as applied in the ancient wisdom literature (1992: 107).

In line with what we have already noted above, he observes that the book begins with an introduction (1:1) and motto (1:2), and ends with the same motto (12:8) and an epilogue (12:9–14). Within the body of the book, like Castellino, he notes the sudden change of style in 5:1 (MT 4:17), but finds that in fact this is only one of several such transitions. The Teacher has two basic styles of discourse and alternates between them.

The first is what de Jong calls 'observations'. Observations are typically introduced by the statements 'I saw' (*r'h*) or 'I know'(*yd'*).[3] The use of the first person predominates. The tone is generally pessimistic, and the accent falls on human impotence. The second, which de Jong calls 'instructions', are characterized by imperatives and second-person indicatives. The tone is more positive, and the accent falls on what is possible and sensible. The Teacher's advice is to be prudent, especially with regard to authority figures and to God. De Jong calls passages in which observations predominate 'observation complexes', and passages in which instruction predominates 'instruction complexes'. The alternation between the two, which occurs throughout the book, is the key to its structure:[4]

1:1	introduction	
1:2	motto	
1:3 – 4:16		observation complex
5:1–9		instruction complex
5:10–6:9		observation complex
6:10–7:22		instruction complex
7:23–29		observation complex
8:1–8		instruction complex
8:9–9:12		observation complex
9:13–12:7		instruction complex
12:8	motto	
12:9–14	epilogue	

These two basic kinds of passages are also distinguished in other ways. The term *hebel* occurs thirty-eight times in the book,[5] but varies in the way it is used. It is a key term in the observation complexes, where it occurs twenty-three times, almost exclusively in the stereotyped conclusions, 'This too is *hebel*', or 'This too is *hebel*, and a chasing after the wind.' In the instruction passages it occurs almost exclusively in arguments; the fact that something is *hebel* forms the basis for a piece of advice or a question. For example, 5:7: 'Much dreaming and many words are *hebel*. Therefore stand in awe of God', or 6:11: 'Where there are many words one multiplies *hebel*. How does

---

[3] Cf. Loader (1979), to whom de Jong acknowledges his indebtedness.

[4] The following table is adapted from de Jong 1992: 108. The verse numbers correspond to those of the NIV and other English versions. The corresponding verse numbers for the MT, as represented in *BHS*, are 1:1 introduction; 1:2 motto; 1:3 – 4:16 observation complex; 4:17 – 5:8 instruction complex; 5:9 – 6:9 observation complex, and thereafter no difference from the NIV.

[5] Eight of them are in the significant frame texts 1:2 and 12:8.

that profit anyone?' (my translations). What de Jong calls the 'enjoyment texts' (which conclude that there is nothing better than eating, drinking and finding satisfaction in one's work) are found only in the observation complexes, and underline, in their own way, the impotence of the individual. The theme of enjoyment is taken up in a different way in 11:7–10, the last instruction complex.

In the observation complexes the theme of human labour is central. The key words are 'toil' (*'ml*) and 'work' (*'śh*), and their derivatives. When used of human labour, these terms occur almost exclusively in the observation passages, where the limitations and unprofitability of such labour are emphasized. That all human endeavour is *heḇel* is the basic conviction of the book.

The other major theme is wisdom. In the observation complexes, the kind of wisdom traditionally associated with Solomon is viewed critically. The instruction complexes, by contrast, affirm its relative advantage over folly. But the common element in all the Teacher's recommendations is *caution*, which is the logical consequence of his observations. The fact of human frailty, which he observes everywhere, compels him to adopt a wisdom of caution.

The distinction between observation and instruction is not absolute. Observation is sometimes found in an instruction passage, and *vice versa*. And the borderline between complexes is often blurred, with transitional passages such as 6:10–11 linking the two. It is the preponderance of one or other of the characteristic styles and its related emphasis that marks a unit, rather than the total absence of alternative elements. The book has 'a wave structure in which observation and instruction often shade off into one another smoothly' (de Jong 1992: 111).

Moreover, while the complexes themselves are reasonably distinct, the structuring of the material within them is often less clear, as is also the case in the book of Proverbs. The main ordering principles appear to be association, opposition and repetition. In Ecclesiastes, repetition, in particular, establishes sub-themes (such as 'time' or 'death') which shed light on the central themes of labour and wisdom.

This analysis by de Jong is valuable in a number of ways. It enables us to begin to catch the main accents of the Teacher's own voice which are heard in the body of the book. It shows how, in terms of his teaching strategies, he belongs firmly within the same broad framework as Israel's other sages. Observation and instruction, association, opposition and repetition were the stock in trade of the wise, in both Israel itself and its wider ancient near-eastern context. But at the same time it alerts us to the distinctively critical and cautious nature of this particular man's teaching, and to the curious way in which he identifies with, and yet maintains a critical distance from, the traditional kind of wisdom associated with Solomon. In short, it provides a plausible account of the book's basic structure and the beginnings of an understanding of how it develops its distinctive themes. It also, incidentally, provides some guidelines for the judicious selection of different kinds of material for closer examination: for example, frame material and core material, observation material and instruction material, expressions highlighted by repetition, and so on. In particular, de Jong's treatment needs to be balanced by close examination of the epilogue, so that the voice of the frame narrator may be clearly heard, and its contribution to the message of the book in its canonical form carefully assessed.

With these considerations in mind, we turn now to examine some passages in more detail. Like a touring party, we shall be able to stop for pictures, so to speak, only here and there. But we shall begin where the book itself does and move on from there, trying to catch some sense of the overall journey on which it takes us, as well as some of its more memorable moments.

Superscription (1:1)

At once we are conducted into the presence of our instructor. We are to sit at the feet of one 'Qohelet, son of David, king in Jerusalem' (my translation). His patronymic ('son of David'), and his title ('king in Jerusalem') place him at the very centre of Israel's political and religious life. But his name, Qohelet, opens up a gap between him and them. For the rest of the Old Testament knows of no such person. The Teacher (as the NIV renders *qōhelet*) is not so much revealed by his name as hidden behind it. The riddle involved in identification and distance, knowing and not knowing, has already begun.

Much more is said about Qohelet in the epilogue, so we shall reserve our main treatment of this issue until then. We simply note three things at this point. First, the word 'Qohelet' (*qōhelet*) is based on the root 'to assemble' (*qhl*). It hints at some official role in the context of an 'assembly' (*qāhāl*). But it is used primarily in Ecclesiastes as a personal name.[6] The article is added (*haqqōhelet*, 'the *qōhelet*') only at

---

[6] Cf. 'Hassoperet' and 'Pokeret' in Ezra 2:55 and 57 respectively, which occur along with other personal names in a list of the servants of Solomon. 'Qohelet' (with or without the article) occurs seven times in all in Ecclesiastes, at 1:1, 2, 12; 7:27; 12:8, 9, 10.

7:27 and 12:8, the latter at a point where the frame narrator wants to exploit the *meaning* of the name as a bridge into the epilogue.[7] Secondly, whether Qohelet is a real name or an artificial one is not clear, though the 'convenience' of its meaning suggests the latter. Finally, it is the frame narrator who introduces Qohelet to us in this cryptic way. He forces us to make what we can of Qohelet ourselves before he himself provides a fuller and more perspicuous description of him at the very end. In other words, who Qohelet is, and how he and his teachings relate to Israel's core beliefs and practices, are issues we are meant to wrestle with through the whole course of the book.

Motto (1:2)

We are still in the hands of the frame narrator here, as the words (literally) 'says Qohelet' remind us. The process of introduction is continuing. We have met the Teacher; now we are given our first taste of his teaching. And the saying the frame narrator has chosen for this purpose takes us directly to its distinctive essence. The first word we hear from Qohelet is *hebel* – 'breath, vapour, mist, vanity, what is transient, ephemeral, profitless'. And as if to establish its key significance for the whole of Qohelet's teaching, it is used no fewer than five times in quick succession: '*hebel* of *hebels* ... *hebel* of *hebels*, everything is *hebel*'.

Eugene Peterson (1992: 153) is surely correct to say that it is a mistake to try to nail this word down, as though one 'right' meaning could be found for it in Ecclesiastes. 'Various meanings glance off [its] surface ... as the context shifts.' It is like the whole category of things it refers to: rootless, unstable, subject to continuous change. But in Qohelet's hands it will become a powerful weapon. For what this motto tells us in no uncertain terms is that Qohelet is a debunker. He will not tolerate pretension, or allow anything to appear more solid or satisfying than it really is. In a delightful image coined by Peterson, he uses *hebel* like a little broom to sweep away all our illusions.[8]

There are dangers in this, of course. In particular, there is a tension between where Qohelet stands – at the centre of Israel's institutions – and the debunking agenda he has set himself. The word 'everything' is so absolute and uncompromising: 'everything (*hakôl*) is *hebel*'. If we

---

[7] The suggestion of the *BHS* critical apparatus regarding *'mrh qhlt* at 7:27 is almost certainly correct and should be adopted, although the reason for the use of the article at this point is not clear.

[8] '... he will drive out from Israel and church all who trade in fraudulent coin, and sweep the place clean with his broom, *hebel*' (Peterson 1992: 154).

are permitted to mix our metaphors, he may cut off the branch on which he is perched and descend into incoherence, or he may succeed in executing a miraculous balancing act, like an acrobat on a high wire. Either way, he appears to be engaged in a form of ideological brinkmanship of which the outcome is uncertain. He certainly has our attention.

The first observation complex (1:3 – 4:16)

In 1:1 we heard the voice of the frame narrator. In 1:2 this was combined with the voice of Qohelet. Here in 1:3 the frame narrator falls silent and we are left listening to Qohelet alone. Of course, since the frame narrator is the author, his unseen hand still guides us. At one point in the middle of the book (7:27), as we have noted, he will speak again very briefly to remind us that he is still there. But, for the most part, until the very end his influence will be exercised only indirectly, through the way he arranges the material he has selected for inclusion.

The central theme: toil

The question of 1:3 forms a bridge into the first observation complex and announces its central theme: the profitability or otherwise of human toil: 'What profit is there for man in all his toil at which he toils under the sun?' (my translation). The question itself will be repeated strategically, with minor variations, at 2:22 and 3:9, and the key term *'āmāl* ('toil') and its cognates will occur no fewer than twenty-four times.[9] We must necessarily deal with this material in a somewhat summary fashion.

The negative refrain: heḇel

First we may note that the entire complex is punctuated by the negative refrain, 'This also is *heḇel* and a chasing after the wind.' It occurs eight times in all, and is the note on which the whole passage ends.[10] This makes the rhetorical purpose very clear. The observations are made in order to establish the thesis announced in the motto of 1:2, that everything is *heḇel* – especially, in this instance, toil. This rhetorical thrust encourages us to try to look for some kind of logical structure in the material, the development of an argument. It may not be the kind of argument to which we are accustomed as modern readers, so we need

---

[9] Twice in each of 1:3; 2:10, 11, 18, 19, 20, 21; and 4:8; once each in 2:24; 3:13; 4:4, 9; and three times in 2:22.

[10] The full refrain occurs in 1:14; 2:11, 17, 26; 4:4, 16. It occurs in an abbreviated form at 1:17, 2:23 and 4:6.

to proceed with due caution. But some connectedness and development of thought may be expected.

Major compositional units

Secondly, at least some major sub-units are clearly discernible. These are the building-blocks out of which the whole complex has been constructed. The poem of 1:4–11 is a distinct unit. The royal testament[11] which begins at 1:12 ('I, [Qohelet], was king over Israel in Jerusalem'), in which wisdom emerges as a sub-theme, reaches its climax in the conclusions drawn from it at the end of chapter 2 (vv. 24–26).[12] In chapters 3 and 4 the situation is more complex. The one apparently distinct unit is the poem on the times in 3:1–8. Immediately after it, however, the key question about toil is restated, and the twin themes of time and toil become interwoven. The first clear sign of closure comes at 4:4–6 with the return of the refrain 'heḇel, and a chasing after the wind'.[13] This makes highly plausible Murphy's suggestion that the whole of 3:1 – 4:6, including the opening poem, constitutes one unit on the twin themes of time and toil. This leaves us with 4:7–16 as the concluding unit of the whole complex. Here toil is brought into connection with a third sub-theme: companionship. The final unit proceeds in a 'one, two, three, many' progression from the solitary man of 4:8 to the youth of 4:16, who had 'all the people' as his apparent supporters. So the central theme (the vanity of toil) is sustained, but it is progressively brought into connection with a number of sub-themes, especially wisdom, time and companionship.

The structure of the argument

Now we must press beyond this to ask how the themes, presented in this manner, support the central thesis that all is heḇel. Again, only basic observations are possible here. We shall revisit some of the key issues later.

The opening poem of 1:4–11 establishes that the physical world is characterized by endless repetition, with no goal being reached, and that human beings have the same character as their environment. As the sea is never filled, neither is the ear. Endless repetition logically excludes the possibility of anything being genuinely new, lasting or

---

[11] Cf. Crenshaw 1987: 29.

[12] While to some extent these verses are a distinct unit, their close thematic connections with what precedes, and the fact that 3:1 is clearly a new beginning, make it natural to see them as the conclusion of the royal testament.

[13] Its first occurrence since the end of ch. 2.

fully satisfying. There can be no profit. Everything is *hebel* in the sense of being transitory, passing, of no lasting significance.

The royal testament which follows is a logical sequel to this, because it illustrates the same general truth by means of an elaborate case study. Allusions to Solomon abound here, without his ever being named. The question of how Qohelet can 'be' Solomon, and yet remain himself, is best explained by recognizing the royal testament for what it is. It is not reportage, but an ironic use of a well-known genre.[14] Kings of the ancient Near East were much given to boasting of their achievements, normally in the form of inscriptions on impressive monuments.[15] It was an unabashed form of self-aggrandisement, and an attempt to achieve an immortality of sorts by ensuring that their name, and the memory of their most impressive accomplishments, lived on after them. Qohelet subverts the genre here by means of a dramatic monologue, in which Solomon's impressive works are systematically recounted, only to have *hebel* written over them all. We might compare Paul's boasting of his weakness in 2 Corinthians 11.[16] For the prophets, the flaw in Solomon's impressive career was his apostasy. For Qohelet, it was his sheer mortality, and the way his awareness of it corroded his enjoyment of what he achieved, even while he still had it. *Hebel* here moves strongly in the direction of 'futility', and does so under the impact of death, mentioned here explicitly for the first time (2:15–16).

The great works reviewed in the royal testament are all done in *wisdom*,[17] and, given the constant allusion to Solomon, this can only amount to a critique of a kind of wisdom teaching and lifestyle which looked to Solomon as its source. We shall need to consider this further at a later point, but it can hardly fail to be a significant part of how Ecclesiastes relates to its wider Old Testament context.

The royal testament spirals down to a point of near suicidal despair ('I hated life', 2:17, cf. 18, 20) before relief finally comes in the closing verses of chapter 2. The possibility of enjoyment returns, significantly, only when the quest for profit is given up altogether (2:22–23), and

---

[14] Seow (1992) has demonstrated that Qoheleth's self-designation is based on the widespread genre of royal inscriptions 'in a way that is contrary to the intent of the typical royal inscription'. Cited in Brown 1996: 122.

[15] E.g. West Semitic royal inscriptions such as the Mesha Inscription (*ANET*: 320–321) and the Kilamuwa Inscription (*ANET*: 654–655). A striking example from the Persian period itself, in which the author of Ecclesiastes probably lived, is the massive Behistun Inscription of Darius I.

[16] Cf. also Shelley's *Ozymandias*, 'king of kings' (Shelley 1943: 550).

[17] The key term *hokmâ* ('wisdom') occurs twelve times across the entire span of the royal testament, in 1:13, 16 (twice), 17, 18; 2:3, 9, 12, 13, 19, 21, 26.

replaced by the notion of gift. Opportunities to eat, drink and find satisfaction in one's work, when they come, are not human achievements but divine gifts, and are to be enjoyed as such (2:24–25). They are only palliatives, to be sure, for they too are *hebel*, and will slip from our grip like everything else – but that is no reason to reject them. As well as lifting the gloom momentarily, these verses provide a bridge into what follows by introducing the idea of God as the sovereign disposer of human fortunes. This issue is brought into sharp focus in chapter 3 in terms of the 'times' of human life (3:1–8).

Here the question of the profitability of human toil is taken up afresh in a much more expressly theological context. The 'time to die', which writes *hebel* over everything, is a time determined by God. But so are all the other times of human life. This means that the worker is never in control, and can never, strictly speaking, achieve anything (3:9). It is God's work, not his, that has enduring significance, and that is something he can neither contribute to nor understand (3:11, 14). The *'ôlām* ('eternity') in the human heart in 3:11 is best understood in terms of what immediately follows in the second half of that verse. It is a God-given awareness that there is something more than the particulars, an overarching scheme of things determined by God: 'all that God has done from beginning to end'. The burden under which the human labourer toils is of knowing that this greater reality exists, without ever being able to see it clearly as God does. And this frustration is deliberately imposed by God so that human beings will always be able to recognize the difference between themselves and their Maker and defer to him: 'God has done it so that men will revere him' (3:14).

This issue of knowing yet not knowing shows itself in a particular way in 3:15 – 4:4 as Qohelet struggles with the fact of rampant injustice in the world. He thinks in his heart (3:17 – a manifestation of the *'ôlām* which God has placed there?) that there must be a time when God will judge, but is unable to affirm that there is anything beyond death (3:18–21). He is suspended between belief in an eschatological moment, a time that will give meaning to all the other times, and agnosticism about the afterlife. This dilemma confirms for him, in its own way, his observation that 'there is nothing better for a man than to enjoy his work, for that is his lot' (3:22).

Qohelet's theological exertions have left him exhausted, and so he finishes on a less ambitious note, with some more or less straightforward observations about the relative value of companionship, especially in the context of toil (4:7–16). Companionship has the capacity to sweeten the bitterness of labour, and even to make some real returns possible (4:9). But, like other good things such as eating and drinking, it is a consolation rather than an answer. We have already noted the 'one, two, three, many' structure of this passage. Companionship is always in danger of collapsing under the weight of numbers (the host of hangers-on of 4:13–16). And when it does fail, the underlying problem emerges again with undiminished force: 'This too is *heḇel*, a chasing after the wind' (4:16).

Angle of vision: 'under the sun'

The expression 'under the sun' occurs in the question that opens this first complex (1:3), and thirteen times in all throughout it.[18] It is unique to Ecclesiastes, and establishes a certain perspective, or angle of vision, for the observations Qohelet makes, not only here, but throughout the entire book. At three points only, all in the first three chapters, it is replaced by the phrase 'under heaven' (1:13; 2:3; 3:1).

It could be that the two expressions are simply synonymous, but it is more likely, in my judgment, that there is a subtle difference. The opening question, 'What does a man gain from all his labour at which he toils under the sun?' (1:3), leads directly, as we have seen, into the poem of 1:4–11. Here the sun is the first element of humankind's physical environment to be mentioned, followed by wind, rivers and seas. It is a poem about the world as an apparently closed system. It seems likely, therefore, that by life 'under the sun' we are meant to understand human existence viewed primarily with reference to the earth as the environment in which men and women live. In contrast, the first occurrence of the expression 'under heaven', in 1:13, is followed immediately by the exclamation, 'What a heavy burden God has laid on men!' This is the first reference to God in the book. Moreover, the connection between God and heaven is underlined strongly in 5:2: 'God is in heaven, and you are on earth.' It is therefore probable that the expression 'under heaven' carries the additional nuance of the divine government of the world in which human beings live.[19]

So the angle of vision varies. We have seen that some parts of the text are much more explicitly theological than others. What is significant, however, is that the verdict of *heḇel* is consistently maintained, whether God's involvement with the world is on view at a particular point or

[18] At 1:3, 9, 14: 2:11, 17, 18, 19, 20; 3:16; 4:1, 3, 7, 15.

[19] Unlike 'under the sun', 'under heaven' is not unique to Ecclesiastes, and is frequently highly charged with notions of divine government; e.g. Gen. 6:17 (the flood), Exod. 17:14 (holy war on Amalek); Deut. 7:24; 9:14; 25:19; 29:20; 2 Kgs. 14:27 (divine decision to save Israel). Cf. the common designation of Yahweh as 'God of heaven', especially in later OT literature, e.g. Ezra 1:2; 5:11; Neh. 1:4–5; Dan. 2:18–19.

not. Belief in God does not relieve the observed and experienced fact of *hebel.*

The first instruction complex (5:1–9)

We shall concentrate only on the first seven verses of chapter 5. Verses 8–9, which are of mixed character, are where this instruction passage begins to merge into the next observation complex (cf. de Jong 1992: 226).

[1] Guard your steps when you go into the house of God. Go near to listen rather than to offer the sacrifice of fools, who do not know that they do wrong.

[2] Do not be quick with your mouth,
    do not be hasty in your heart
    to utter anything before God.
  God is in heaven
    and you are on earth,
    so let your words be few.
[3] As a dream comes when there are many cares,
    so the speech of a fool when there are many words.

[4] When you make a vow to God, do not delay in fulfilling it. He has no pleasure in fools; fulfil your vow. [5] It is better not to vow than to make a vow and not fulfil it. [6] Do not let your mouth lead you into sin. And do not protest to the ... messenger, 'My vow was a mistake.' Why should God be angry at what you say and destroy the work of your hands? [7] Much dreaming and many words are meaningless. Therefore stand in awe of [fear] God.

After the long observation complex of chapters 1 – 4 the change of style here is abrupt and striking. Qohelet has moved into a different mode of discourse. But the conceptual links with what has gone before are almost equally striking. The all-pervasive theme of human toil is resumed in the expression, 'the work of your hands' (5:6). The purpose statement of 3:14, 'God does it so that men will fear him', finds its counterpart here in the exhortation, 'Therefore fear God' (5:7, my translations). And the presentation of God as creator, disposer and judge in chapters 2 – 3 provides the basis for the warnings now given about trifling with him.

The repeated reference to fools indicates, by implication, that this is a piece of instruction in the kind of wisdom that Qohelet himself advocates. De Jong's designation of it as a wisdom of caution is certainly borne out by this passage.[20] It is based, negatively, on a recognition of the transience and futility of everything earthly, and especially of the attempts of human beings to achieve anything of lasting significance by their own efforts. Positively, it rests on a recognition of the absolute transcendence of God, and of his power and right to judge.

But there are strong suggestions here that human beings have not been left altogether in the dark about what this God requires of them. Foolish behaviour is not simply a matter of talking too much (5:7), but of failing to *listen* (5:1), which implies revelation. Furthermore, the exhortations about vow-keeping here presuppose the instruction on this matter in the Torah.[21] To go to the house of God to *listen* is to go there to hear the revealed will of God expounded in the form of Torah, and wisdom is to conform one's behaviour to it. Human beings may not be able to read the book of creation (3:11), but they can read, or at least listen to, the book of the Torah.

In general, the positive conclusion drawn from the exposé of human frailty and futility in the preceding observation complex is that human beings should fear God. And fearing God is tied, by implication, to attentiveness to his Torah.

With this understanding of the logical connection between observation and instruction in the body of the book, we are ready to move to chapter 12, to see how the whole work is brought to its conclusion.

The final poem (12:1–7)

¹ Remember your Creator
    in the days of your youth,
  before the days of trouble come
    and the years approach when you will say,
     'I find no pleasure in them' –
² before the sun and the light
    and the moon and the stars grow dark,
    and the clouds return after the rain;
³ when the keepers of the house tremble,
    and the strong men stoop ...

---

[20] A more venturesome aspect of it will appear later, however, esp. in 11:1–6.

[21] Num. 30, and esp. Deut. 23:21–23.

[6] ... before the silver cord is severed,
  or the golden bowl is broken;
 before the pitcher is shattered at the spring,
  or the wheel broken at the well,
[7] and the dust returns to the ground it came from,
  and the spirit returns to God who gave it.

Context

The exhortation to 'Remember', which opens this poem corresponds to the 'Guard your steps' and 'Go near to listen' of 5:1. In terms of de Jong's 'wave structure', it completes the final instruction complex.[22] More particularly, it completes the discourse on youth and old age which began in 11:7.[23]

Structure

After the opening exhortation, the content of the poem is structured by the repetition of 'before' (*'aḏ '"šer lō '*) in verses 1, 2 and 6:

> Remember your Creator
>   before the days of trouble (v. 1b)[24]
> before old age (vv. 2–5)
> before death (v. 6).

The expression 'days of trouble', which is very general, is specified in 12:2–6 as days of advancing age and death.

Development of thought

'Remember your Creator' implies relationship and obligation. It picks up all the references to creation in the body of the book and brings them to a sharp point of application. There is no conflict in Qohelet's teaching between enjoyment of life and recognition of God; indeed, they are inextricably linked. God as creator lays down the parameters within which life is to be enjoyed. What is involved in 'remembering' him is not spelled out here, and must be deduced from earlier samples of Qohelet's instruction, especially 5:1–7. The stress here in chapter 12

---

[22] The complex began in 9:13. In terms of the frame which encloses the body of the book, 12:1–7 is the counterpart of the opening poem of 1:4–11, as we noted earlier. That poem observed as a simple fact the endless passing of the generations. This one calls for a particular response from each individual in view of the relentless approach of death.

[23] In the Hebrew text it is expressly linked to what has gone before by the conjunction 'and': 'And remember' (*úz"ḵōr*).

[24] The 'days of trouble' stand in contrast to 'the days of your youth' in 12:1a.

falls on the urgency of doing so while one can, for just as the opportunity for enjoyment will pass, so too will the opportunity for remembering God.

Old age, like youth, is decreed by God (7:14; 11:7–10), and is presented here in a succession of striking images. It is like a persistently overcast and rainy day (12:2). The first evil of old age is the absence of any prospect of recovery. The second image, extended and allegorical, is of a decaying house (12:3–4a). Then, in a flurry of mixed metaphors, the old person is pictured on the move, slowly, laboriously, and anxiously, to his final destination (12:4b–5).[25] The silver cord and golden bowl, and the pitcher suspended over the well, depict life in all its fragile beauty and wholesome simplicity, and 'broken' represents the shattering finality of death (12:6). And this is a judgment imposed on human beings by God, for the closing verse of the poem is a transparent allusion to Genesis 3:19: 'dust you are and to dust you will return'.

There is a tantalizing opaqueness about the double 'return' of verse 7 ('the dust returns to the ground ... and the spirit returns to God'), which relates to the vexed question of the afterlife and the possibility of a final judgment to redress the wrongs that have gone unchecked in this world. 'Know that for all these things God will bring you to judgment' (11:9) suggests a judgment more particular and discriminating than death. But 'man goes to his eternal home' (12:5) implies that death is the absolute end. There is a stubborn ambiguity here, which cannot be resolved by intense scrutiny of these statements. Neither can it be clarified by recourse to Qohelet's earlier observations and instructions. The same issue emerged, as we saw, in chapter 3, and was left unresolved there too. Moreover, it is entirely in keeping with Qohelet's 'wisdom of caution' that he leaves it that way. He will not exceed the bounds God has imposed on him. He ends by confronting us, as he has done all the way through, with the reality of death itself as a divine judgment, and by calling on us to remember God and enjoy his gifts while we have the opportunity to do so.

Motto (12:8)

'Utter *heḇel*', says Qohelet, 'everything is *heḇel*' (my translation). We have already noted the structural significance of this verse as a bridge between the body of the book and the epilogue of verses 9–14.[26] The

---

[25] 'Eternal home' (*bêṯ 'ôlam*) in 12:5 is a play on 'house' (*bayiṯ*) in 12:3.

[26] The occurrence of the article here with Qohelet, literally 'the Qohelet', points forward to the description of his public role as a teacher of 'the people' in 12:9–12.

frame narrator's voice returns here in the expression, 'says Qohelet'. We have already re-entered the frame of the book with the poem of 12:1–7. Now we do so more explicitly. With the frame narrator's help, we take one step back and begin to view Qohelet more objectively.

It remains simply to note that in its last occurrence here *hebel* comes freighted with all the connotations it has acquired in the course of the book: transience, futility, incomprehensibility and so on. But the final colouring it has acquired is from the description of life as a 'silver cord' and a 'golden bowl' in 12:6. Life is precious precisely because, like breath, it is *hebel* – fragile, fleeting, transient. The connotations of *hebel* in Ecclesiastes are not wholly negative.[27]

The epilogue (12:9–14)

⁹Not only was [Qohelet] wise, [he constantly taught the people knowledge. He weighed] and searched out and set in order many proverbs. ¹⁰[He sought to find desirable words], and what he wrote was upright and true.

¹¹The words of the wise are like goads, their collected sayings like firmly embedded nails – given by one Shepherd. ¹²[Of anything beyond these beware, my son.]

Of making many books there is no end, and much study wearies the body.

> ¹³ [The end of the matter, all has been heard:]
>   Fear God, and keep his commandments,
>   [this is the essence of being human;]
> ¹⁴ For God will bring every deed into judgment,
>   including every hidden thing,
>   whether it is good or evil.[28]

Now the only voice we hear, as at the beginning, is that of the frame narrator. He first reflects on Qohelet himself (12:9–10), and then on 'the wise' in general (12:11–12). The words 'The end of the matter', in verse 13, in effect bring down the final curtain. They set off the last two verses as the conclusion, not just to the epilogue, but to the book as a whole. The writer of the epilogue addresses us as his 'son' (12:12) in the manner of a conventional wise man,[29] and treats us to a blend of

---

[27] Cf. Fredericks 1993: ch. 1. Fredericks argues convincingly, in my judgment, that the primary connotation of *hebel* in Ecclesiastes is not futility but transience.

[28] Phrases in square brackets are my translation.

[29] 'Son' here is a traditional term for 'pupil'.

information, warning and exhortation.

The critical issue for us as we come to 'the end of the matter' is the relationship between the voice we hear now and the one we have been listening to in the body of the book. Put another way, it is the question of how the epilogue interprets Qohelet's teaching and calls upon us to respond to it.

First, the epilogue assures us that Qohelet was not merely a private (perhaps eccentric) sage, but one who exercised a sustained and responsible public role (12:9a). It attests to his skill in weighing, searching out and arranging his material, and affirms that the result ('what he wrote', *kātûb*) was upright and true, and belongs to the wider corpus of Israelite wisdom (12:9b–11). The warning of verse 12 is not against the teaching of Qohelet and the other recognized sages, but what is 'in addition to' or 'beyond' them. The 'one Shepherd' of 12:11 is best understood as a reference to God as the ultimate source and guarantor of Israel's wisdom.[30]

Secondly, and paradoxically, the epilogue recognizes, by implication, that Qohelet's teaching in a sense illustrates the very futility of which he speaks. The proverb at the end of 12:12, 'Of making many books there is no end, and much study wearies [*yg'*] the body', echoes something that was said at the very beginning: 'All things are wearisome [*yg'*], more than one can say' (1:8).[31] Qohelet's teaching falls at the weary edge of Israel's wisdom, where grappling with unanswerable questions brings exhaustion. Beyond this it is not safe to go.

Thirdly, it points us to the one thing that remains when wisdom of the searching, enquiring kind has reached its limits, namely, the fear of God, which consists of keeping his commandments. The term 'commandments' (*miṣwôt*) appears here for the first time, but we have already noted the allusions to the Torah in chapter 5. And although Qohelet himself has recommended enjoyment of life, this has been qualified by injunctions like 'guard', 'listen', and 'remember', which imply obedience to known requirements. In this the epilogue simply makes explicit what Qohelet himself has taught by implication.

Finally, the epilogue revisits the question of judgment and affirms that God will judge in a way that will bring everything hidden to light

---

[30] The 'one Shepherd' has variously been identified as Solomon, Moses, Qohelet himself, God, or simply (by Fox 1977: 102–103) as 'a (any) shepherd'. Among recent interpreters, Murphy (1992: 125) is one who favours the identification with God. For my part, the bracketing references to God in 12:1, 13–14, are decisive.

[31] Cf. also 1:15, 'What is twisted cannot be straightened; what is lacking cannot be counted', and 1:18, 'With much wisdom comes much sorrow; the more knowledge, the more grief.'

and discriminate between good and evil. This does not resolve Qohelet's personal dilemma about the afterlife; there is no explicit statement about that here either. It simply affirms that what Qohelet thought in his heart in 3:17, and boldly asserted in 11:9, is indeed the case, and leaves it at that: God will judge. What is hidden must remain so until God himself brings it to light. In the meantime, fearing God and keeping his commandments is what enables a person to live with *hebel* without being overwhelmed by it. It is 'the whole' of what it means to be human (*kol-hā'āḏām*, v. 13).

Overall, the effect of the voice we hear in the epilogue is to inculcate respect for Qohelet and to guide us to the conclusion the frame narrator wants us to draw from his teaching.[32] I have tried to argue that this is not an artificial conclusion to the book, but one that emerges naturally from Qohelet's own train of thought.[33]

II

Now at last we may turn our attention to broader issues. At the outset we noted that the way Qohelet was introduced to us in chapter 1 implicitly raised the issue of his relationship to Israel's traditional beliefs and practices, especially those associated with Solomon. If the book has the kind of unity for which I have argued, I can now pose this same basic question in a more holistic way in line with the particular terms of reference I have set myself. My purpose in what follows is not

---

[32] Longman (1998), following Fox (1977), has argued that the author of the epilogue subtly critiques Qohelet's teaching in 12:9–11 before turning the reader's attention away from it towards foundational, orthodox truths of Israel's faith in 12:12–14. But this requires a twofold departure from the MT in 12:10. The Qal passive participle *kāṯûḇ* has to be emended to the infinitive absolute *kāṯôḇ*, which must then be read as standing for the infinitive construct *kᵉṯôḇ*. The resultant translation, 'Qohelet sought ... to write honestly words of truth', opens the door to Longman's view that the writer effectively damns Qohelet with faint praise: he *sought* to write words of truth, but did not always succeed in doing so. This translation is highly questionable, however, and a far cry from what the MT as it stands actually says. This is accurately reflected in the NIV translation: 'what he wrote was upright and true' (cf. NRSV, NEB). Also, and more importantly, Longman fails to do justice to the fundamental agreement between the conclusion drawn in 12:12–14 and the key elements of Qohelet's own thought in the body of the book (esp. in chs. 3 and 5) to which I have drawn attention.

[33] This is demonstated in a particular way by the manner in which the epilogue functions in its immediate context in ch. 12. This final chapter of the book contains words of both Qohelet and the frame narrator. It begins with God as creator (v. 1) and ends with him as lawgiver and judge (vv. 13–14). Between these is God, the one Shepherd, who guides his people through the wisdom he gives to men like Qohelet (v. 11).

to try to reconstruct Qohelet's historical and social context (although I may touch on this incidentally), but to address the literary and theological question: how does the *book* of Ecclesiastes relate to its Old Testament context? What is its special contribution to the wider discourse in which it participates as part of the Hebrew canon? Our survey of key parts of the book has already glanced at this in a variety of ways. Now it is time to draw the threads together. Much could be said, but we shall concentrate here on three major issues, starting with how Ecclesiastes draws on traditional beliefs about creation, since this is foundational to its entire worldview.

Ecclesiastes and Genesis 1 – 11

In Ecclesiastes God is supremely the creator, and the particular ways in which his relationship to the world and to humankind are understood throughout the book appears to draw heavily on the early chapters of Genesis. God is 'the Maker of all things' (11:5), and 'your Creator' (12:1). In particular, he made human beings upright, though they have gone in search of many schemes (7:29). This is probably an allusion to the creation of human beings in the image of God and their subsequent fall, as in Genesis 1 – 3. This is made virtually certain by references to man being made from dust and destined to return to it (3:20; 12:7; cf. Gen. 2:7; 3:19). The wording here is so close to that of Genesis that direct dependence seems undeniable.

Furthermore, the view that God has 'made everything beautiful in its time' (3:11) may allude to the creation account of Genesis 1. The recognition that there is knowledge and wisdom which God has placed beyond human reach (3:11; 7:23) may reflect Genesis 2, with its teaching about the forbidden tree (a tree to be desired to make one wise). And finally, the teaching of Ecclesiastes that there is a crookedness in the world which God has put there and which human beings are powerless to remove (7:13), and that frustrating toil is a 'heavy burden' that God has placed on human beings (1:13; 3:10), suggests that the fall narrative of Genesis 3 is, once again, not far below the surface.[34] As in Genesis, God is judge and the one who determines the conditions of human existence on earth precisely because he is first of all creator.

Qohelet does not simply repeat the teaching of Genesis, however, but works with it in his own distinctive way, and we shall note in a moment

---

[34] Cf. also 3:11, where 'eternity' in the heart may be an allusion to the creation of human beings in the image of God (the eternal one).

how he does so. It certainly appears to play a foundational role in his thinking.[35] Indeed it may not be going too far to assert with C. C. Forman (1956: 263) that 'the early chapters of Genesis represent the single most important influence on the ideas of Ecclesiastes regarding the nature and destiny of man, the character of human existence, and the fact of God'.[36] The theology of Ecclesiastes is grounded firmly in traditional Israelite beliefs about such matters.

What is particularly significant for us to note here is that Qohelet's most distinctive teaching, that everything is *hebel*, must be understood against this background. *Hebel* is not simply a brute fact, something which happens to be there without cause or explanation. It is a judgment, a condition, imposed on the world, and on human beings in particular, by God. It is a manifestation of the fall and, positively, of God's rule as creator and judge.

This provides an important key for understanding the relationship between Ecclesiastes and the kind of wisdom traditionally associated with Solomon.

Ecclesiastes and Proverbs

The way the epilogue locates Qohelet in the mainstream of Israelite wisdom should warn us against seeing his teaching as a direct attack on Solomonic wisdom, especially in the canonical form in which we have it in the book of Proverbs. Yet clearly there is a tension between them that is evident in the body of the book, as we have seen, and which cannot be ignored in any responsible reading of it. The difference relates essentially to the way the doctrine of creation functions in the two works.

In Ecclesiastes the inferences drawn from creation are essentially deterministic. The creator of the world is also the one who has made the times, the bad ones as well as the good (7:14). But since he has also set severe limits to human knowledge (3:11), his ways remain incomprehensible to human beings, who are therefore never in a position to secure guaranteed outcomes for particular kinds of behaviour. There are good things to be enjoyed, and commandments to

[35] It may even be that the term *hebel*, as Qohelet uses it, was suggested by the name of Abel (*hebel*) in Genesis. 'Abel's brief life is the life of Everyman' (Forman 1956: 258, citing MacDonald 1933: 111). Cf. Ellul 1990: 58–59; Brown 1996: 131 n. 33.

[36] However, Forman himself (contrary to me) thinks that, in one respect at least, Qohelet's thought diverges from that of Genesis: 'There is in Genesis a hint that God is not omniscient, for "he was sorry that he had made man ..." (cf. vi 6f). Koheleth did not share this suspicion about the deity' (1956: 263).

be obeyed, but notions of success and profit are logically excluded. Human beings experience life in the world as *hebel*.

The concept of creation is equally important in the book of Proverbs, but it is less obviously influenced by the specifics of Genesis 1 – 3. It moves in a different direction, and the implications are more open-ended and positive. The great poem of Proverbs 8:22–30 establishes, as basic to the teaching of the whole book, that the entire created order is an expression of the wisdom of God (cf. 3:19–20). From this comes a confidence that careful observation and attentiveness to one's teachers can enable a person to gain wisdom that is genuinely useful in attaining a happy and successful life (3:1–18). Ultimately this is understood in terms of divine blessing rather than of human achievement (10:22; 3:17), but the way God works in his world is taken to be sufficiently consistent and understandable to make good living more profitable than bad. Human beings experience life as a choice (or series of choices) between two ways, and how they fare is largely determined by the choices they make (12:28; 14:12; 16:25).

These two works are certainly in tension, but not in fundamental conflict if we attend to them carefully. Proverbs acknowledges that, in the end, it is God, not human beings, who determines the outcome of events: 'In his heart a man plans his course, but the LORD determines his steps' (16:9); 'The lot is casts into the lap, but its every decision is from the LORD' (16:33). And Ecclesiastes, as we have seen, acknowledges the relative advantage of wisdom over folly (2:13; 10:12). They are both anchored in creation theology, and the fear of God is the essence of wisdom for both of them. Proverbs begins with it (1:7) and Ecclesiastes ends with it (12:13).[37] Rightly understood, the difference is one of emphasis. The special contribution of Ecclesiastes is to insist on the presence of *hebel* as a universal datum of human experience which must be acknowledged, and to rule out of court any kind of wisdom teaching that refuses to do this – *even if its practitioners claim to be disciples of Solomon*. It guards wisdom against unreality.[38]

---

[37] In this connection Proverbs uses the name Yahweh, while Ecclesiastes speaks only of the fear of God (Elohim). But too much should not be made of this. Both terms occur in the creation accounts of Gen. 1 – 2, and both Proverbs and Ecclesiastes, like the wisdom literature in general, have a 'cosmopolitan' rather than a narrowly Israelite focus.

[38] Cf. Brown (1996: 135): 'Inflated and ambitious goals, pretentious claims of knowledge, obsessive concerns for getting ahead are all exposed for what they are in the face of the absurdity of life, mere delusions of grandeur. Life's grand purposes are whittled down to simple, fleeting pleasures.' Brown describes Qohelet's orientation to

Ecclesiastes and the Feast of Tabernacles

The question of the special character of Ecclesiastes, and therefore what to do with it, clearly troubled Israel in the first century AD. Its inspiration was a matter of hot dispute among the Pharisees, with some advocating that it be 'stored away' (removed from public use). The school of Shammai denied its inspiration, partly on the ground of alleged heretical tendencies, while the school of Hillel defended it. But the verdict went in its favour at Jamnia, and with the subsequent decline of the school of Shammai its position was beyond dispute.[39]

Its eventual incorporation into the Feast of Tabernacles (or Booths) shows just how thoroughly Israel has recognized its worth and taken its message to heart. For the Feast of Tabernacles stands in the mainstream of Israel's religious life, along with the other two great festivals, Passover and Weeks (Deut. 16:16). It is essentially a joyful autumn festival, lasting seven days, and celebrating the end of the agricultural year, when the produce of the wheat and grape harvests has been gathered in (Deut. 23:13–17). At the same time, it recalls the very different circumstances of Israel's ancestors, who dwelt in temporary shelters (booths) in the wilderness, on the way to this land of plenty (Lev. 23:43; Roth 1971: 1058).[40]

It is perhaps paradoxical that so sombre a book should be read at so joyous a festival, but it shows that Ecclesiastes has a vital role in relation to Israel's explicitly religious life as well as in its wisdom teaching. It keeps joy anchored in reality by injecting the lessons of the wilderness into the celebration of harvest. For in the wilderness the Israelites learned about their human frailty: that their lives were a mere breath, and that to fear God and keep his commandments constituted the whole meaning of their existence. It was a lesson they needed to hear again in the context of harvest celebration, lest being able to eat and drink and find satisfaction in their work should be mistaken for an

---

life as 'minimalist': 'The simple life, without great and glorious ambitions, however noble, is Qoheleth's ideal, a life of simple sufficiency in which constructive work, sufficient food, and fellowship are all that is needed to live life fully' (1996: 136). Cf. also, on a broader front, Holmgren 1999: 107–110. Holmgren argues that one of the main ongoing values of the OT *as a whole* is that 'These Old Testament books guard the Christian community from becoming unreal in its response to life's afflictions.'

[39] The course of rabbinic discussions regarding Ecclesiastes is discussed in detail by Beckwith 1985: esp. 275–302.

[40] Ecclesiastes is read on the intermediate Sabbath of the festival, or on the final day if that is a Sabbath. It is read at the morning service, before the reading of the Torah.

accomplishment rather than a gift, and lead them away from God rather than to him. It was a danger against which the Torah itself warned them (Deut. 6:10–12; 8:10–20). To be reminded of *hebel*, however, is good for the soul, and a vital ingredient in true worship.

III

The message of Ecclesiastes is confronting, and it would be natural to hope that the New Testament, and the gospel in particular, might free us from it. But such is not the case. The New Testament does not annul the teaching of Ecclesiastes, but (and here is the good news) it does not leave it exactly as it is either. As Derek Kidner has put it with delightful succinctness, 'the New Testament upholds the verdict of "vanity", while deepening and broadening our understanding of it' (1985: 115).

The clearest link comes in Paul's classic exposition of the gospel in the letter to the Romans, especially 8:19–24:

> The creation waits in eager expectation for the sons of God to be revealed. For the creation was subjected to frustration [*mataiotēs*], not by its own choice, but by the will of the one who subjected it, in hope that the creation itself will be liberated from its bondage to decay and brought into the glorious freedom of the children of God.
>
> We know that the whole creation has been groaning as in the pains of childbirth right up to the present time. Not only so, but we ourselves, who have the firstfruits of the Spirit, groan inwardly as we wait eagerly for our adoption as sons, the redemption of our bodies. For in this hope we were saved. But hope that is seen is no hope at all. Who hopes for what he already has?

There is no quotation from Ecclesiastes here, but the structure of thought is very similar: creation, the fall,[41] the divine imposition of 'frustration', and the universal experience of it, by unbelievers and believers alike, right up to the 'present time'. In Paul's *mataiotēs* ('frustration'), we have Qohelet's *hebel* in its New Testament dress. It is recognizably the same, but is also changed by being set in a new light. While Qohelet sets it in the light of creation, Paul sets it in the

---

[41] By implication.

light of creation *and redemption*. The 'hope' that transforms *hebel* is the hope of the final release of the whole creation that will come with the manifestation of the sons of God, which is explained in terms of 'the redemption of our bodies'. In this perspective *hebel* becomes a present reality that is still very painful but which, like the pain of childbirth, will finally give way to joy.

Two things are to be noted. First, the 'hope' mentioned here is the hope offered to us in the gospel Paul has been expounding in the previous chapters, which is sealed to our hearts by the Spirit, who marks us as the very 'sons of God' of which the passage speaks (8:12–17). Paul implies that this hope has always existed, or at least has existed as long as the futility itself. God is the author of both. He subjected the creation to futility *in hope*, possibly an allusion to the *proto-euangelion* of Genesis 3:15. But what Romans as a whole implies, and what is stated elsewhere in the New Testament, is that this hope has been fully manifested in Christ and the gospel. Death has been abolished and life and immortality have been brought to light through the gospel (2 Tim. 1:10). The resurrection of Jesus from the dead decisively resolves the ambiguity we found in Ecclesiastes about the afterlife and final judgment (Acts 17:31).

Secondly, this hope, by its very nature, is eschatological. We have the firstfruits of the Spirit, but not yet the full harvest, and we continue to groan along with the rest of creation. The release from *hebel* is not yet. Because, in Ecclesiastes, the certainty that God will judge is mingled with uncertainty about the afterlife, the hope of an eventual release from *hebel* is clouded. In the New Testament the cloud is removed, but there is still the insistence on *hebel* as a present reality. And as long as that remains as part of authentic gospel proclamation, Ecclesiastes will remain an indispensable part of Holy Scripture. For unreality is just as much a danger under the new covenant as it was under the old.

There is one final thing that needs to be said, however, and it is good news. With the gospel comes not just a brighter hope, but a new kind of *work* in which we are called to participate. It is what Paul calls 'the work of Christ' (Phil. 2:30), or 'the work of the Lord' (1 Cor. 16:10; 2 Cor. 15:58). This partakes of the power of the resurrection and the life of the world to come, precisely because it is not our work, but God's. And to the extent that we are engaged in it, in whatever form, we can be sure that this, at least, is not futile. For in this work, the future, in which there is no longer any *hebel*, is already breaking in. 'Therefore, my dear brothers, stand firm. Let nothing move you. Always give yourselves fully to the work of the Lord, because you know that your labour in the Lord is not in vain' (1 Cor. 15:58).

Early in this study we pictured Qohelet as an acrobat on a high wire. We have watched in awe as he has maintained a precarious balance between affirmation and denial, stout orthodoxy and near heresy, and we must applaud him for his performance. But acrobatics is not what he, or the book as a whole, would have us do ourselves. Qohelet's performance is to be learned from rather than imitated. Ecclesiastes is a garment to wear when we have finished with performance and are ready for work – not with an inflated idea of what we can achieve, but with contentment and confidence, knowing that our times are in God's hands. A pair of overalls, perhaps. A garment for those who are through, once for all, with triumphalism and cant, and are willing to face life as it really is.

Chapter Five

Esther

Garment of deliverance

The most important thing about the people of God
is that they *are*. They *exist*.
Eugene Peterson[1]

We began these studies with the Song of Songs, which is read at Passover, the first festival in Israel's liturgical year.[2] With Esther we have come almost full circle. For Esther is the scroll for Purim, which falls just one month before Passover.[3] So Purim and Passover stand back to back; when Purim is celebrated, Passover is just around the corner.

They are two very different kinds of festivals. Purim is noisy, merry and secular in flavour. Passover is calm, meditative and deeply religious. Yet they are linked by a common theme. The Passover celebrates the deliverance of the Israelites from slavery in Egypt, Purim their deliverance from annihilation in Persia. Between them they frame almost the entire sweep of Old Testament history, and mark it as a story of deliverance from beginning to end.

In the case of Esther, the connection between the book and the festival is written into the sacred text itself. The scroll explains the origin of the festival and prescribes the time and manner of its observance. Its purpose is to ensure that 'Jews everywhere and in all generations should celebrate Purim' (Fox 1991: 3). It was therefore almost inevitable that, in time, the reading of the scroll should become a central element of the festival.[4] The theme of the book, like that of the festival itself, is deliverance.

---

[1] Peterson 1992: 236.

[2] Passover is held on 14 Nisan, the first month: Exod. 12:1–2.

[3] On 14 and 15 Adar, the twelfth month: Est. 9:21.

[4] Esther is read at both the evening and morning services of Purim: Roth et al. 1971: 1058.

I

Our first task, as in our earlier studies, is to try to catch the distinctive voice of Esther; to observe its shape and development as a complete work in its own right. Our concern here will be with the book as it appears in the Masoretic Text, though we shall have occasion to refer at one point to the expansions it receives in the Septuagint.[5] In a sense, it has been premature to announce its theme in advance. But that may be forgiven in this case, for the theme is obvious and uncontroversial. What is of particular interest is the way that theme is developed here. How is deliverance in Esther different from deliverance in, say, the exodus, or Judges, or the Joseph narrative?

Esther as story

The fact that Esther, like Ruth, is a narrative work of considerable artistry and complexity has important implications for how it 'works' as literature. Its historicity, and the related question of its genre, are still under discussion in the scholarly world, and no consensus has yet emerged. The genre terms most in vogue in recent years are 'novella' and 'historical romance', terms which associate Esther with extra-canonical works such as Judith and Tobit. But at the same time most scholars use such genre classifications in a carefully qualified way. J. D. Levenson, in his recent commentary, captures the current mood reasonably well:

> ... the book of Esther is best seen as a historical novella set within the Persian empire. This is not to say that the book is false, only that its truth, like the truth of any piece of literature, is relative to its genre, and the genre of Esther is not that of the historical annal (though it sometimes imitates the style of an historical annal) (1997: 25).[6]

David Clines prefers the term 'romance' for Esther, but is more open to the possibility of its having a strong historical base:

---

[5] The expanded Esther of the LXX is canonical for those of Eastern Orthodox persuasion, while the Vulgate is canonical for Roman Catholics. This includes the LXX expansions, translated into Latin and placed in a block at the end. For other Christians, as for Jews, the canonical Esther is the form it has in the MT.

[6] Cf. Fox 1991: 132 n. 4 (to which Levenson refers).

The book of Esther has all the hallmarks of a romance (coincidences, engaging characterisations, etc.) but it can at no point be unequivocally faulted on historical grounds. Much of its historical detail can be substantiated and the supposed errors it contains can be satisfactorily explained. Historians are compelled in such circumstances to trust their own judgment of the kind of literature which lies before them, in the absence of any specific data that settle the question one way or the other (1991: 136).

Given this situation, the judgment of any particular reader, historian or not, is bound to be determined in the end by his or her pre-suppositions about the nature and authority of the Old Testament as a whole. But even the most theologically conservative reader cannot escape the fact that Esther is far from being a mere chronicle. If it is history (and I for one am prepared to accept that it is), it is history as story rather than history as chronicle. It is this artistic quality of the book, its narrativity, to which genre terms such as 'romance' and 'novella' point. They remind us that if we are serious about wanting to engage with Esther and hear its distinctive voice, we must read it as a story, even if our particular theological tradition requires us to read it as a 'having happened in history' story rather than a fictional one. Whether the author's omniscience in relation to the characters and events is the product of his creative imagination or of divine inspiration (or of a combination of these) matters little in terms of the literary nature of the text and the way it must be read to appreciate its message. Genre classifications draw attention to certain features which a particular work has in common with others. It would be unwise, however, to attach more significance to them than this, and in particular they should not be used as a basis for making judgments on matters such as historicity or inspiration, which must be settled on other grounds. Furthermore, when these matters *have* been settled to any particular reader's satisfaction, the basic task of reading still remains, and at this stage it does not greatly matter what genre classification we adopt as long as we are sensitive to the obvious artistry of the text. No genre classification so far proposed is sufficiently precise or secure to constrain reading, beyond this, in any significant way.[7]

---

[7] For a recent critical review of the options see Fox 1991: ch. 4.

Plot

The first feature of the story to which we must give our attention is its plot, for the plot is what carries and integrates all its other elements. Situation, characters and theme are all called into existence and set in their proper relationships to each other by the plot as it progressively unfolds. The plot undergirds and sustains everything else.

In this case the plot is relatively straightforward. The main action does not begin until chapter 3, with the promotion of Haman and the royal proclamation that everyone should bow to him. But this is preceded by an introduction ('exposition' in literary parlance)[8] in which we are given all the information we need in order to understand what follows. In particular, the first two chapters position Esther and Mordecai for the key roles they are to play in the ensuing story. When the crisis breaks, Esther will be in a position to act because she is queen (2:17; 4:14), and Mordecai because his name has been recorded in the book of memorable deeds (2:22–23; 6:1–2). These opening chapters also introduce us to the ethos of the Persian court: an opulent, multilingual world; a world of latent anti-Semitism (2:10), where the king's whim is law and where the law is irreversible (1:19). All these factors, though we may not realize it at the time, are highly significant for the way the plot will unfold. For example, much of the tension of the main action will revolve around the question of how the irreversible can be reversed (cf. Clines 1984: 17ff.).

The crisis that breaks in chapter 3 is not totally resolved until 9:19, where the last of the enemies of the Jews have been destroyed. But there are resting-points, points of partial resolution, along the way. Haman himself has been disposed of by the end of chapter 7, but the problem of the decree he has persuaded the king to issue remains. The solution to this appears in chapter 8 in the form of a second decree authorizing the Jews to defend themselves, and the elevation of Mordecai to the place of power that Haman had formerly occupied. The Jews rightly sense that the situation has turned decisively in their favour and that their future is now secure (8:17b). The feasting and celebration with which this chapter ends mark this as a significant point of resolution. But the logic of the plot will not allow the story to finish here either.[9] The second decree has specified a day on which the Jews

---

[8] Cf. Alter 1981: 80; Ryken 1979: 58; Bush 1996: 300.

[9] Clines (1984: ch. 7) has argued on textual and literary grounds that the book originally ended here and that the whole of chs. 9 and 10 are secondary. Whatever their merits, the particulars of that argument lie beyond the scope of our present discussion,

will be permitted to defend themselves, to destroy their attackers (8:11), and to avenge themselves on their enemies (8:13). This creates considerable suspense, requiring some account of the events of the fateful thirteenth day, even if the outcome is a now a foregone conclusion. In other words, the end of chapter 8 may be *decisive* for the outcome, but it is what follows in 9:1–19 that ties up the loose ends and brings the main action to its final point of rest.

The balance of chapter 9 is an appendix showing how the festival of Purim arose out of the events just described, with 9:19 acting as a bridge between this 'Purim appendix' and the story itself. The work is then rounded off with a short epilogue about Mordecai's high office and beneficent rule (10:1–3). This is a fitting conclusion to the book, for the exalted Mordecai speaks 'peace' (shalom, total well-being) to all his people. This reminds us that deliverance is not simply the removal of threat. It is restoration to a state of complete wholeness, and what better symbol of that could there be than the magnificent Mordecai himself?[10]

The basic design of the book, then, as indicated by the development of its plot, is as follows:

Exposition	chs. 1 – 2
Main action	3:1 – 9:19
Purim appendix	9:20–32
Epilogue	ch. 10

Refinements are possible, of course. David Clines (1984) divides the exposition into seven scenes, and the main action into nine. Michael Fox (1991) divides the book as a whole into a series of acts, each with two or more scenes.[11] Such analyses are helpful in drawing attention to the dramatic quality of the story, but are for the most part incidental to the way the central theme develops.

More significant is the way the plot is structured to some extent around three rounds of feasting, at the beginning (1:1–9; 2:18; 3:15), in the middle (5:1–8; 7:1–9; 8:17), and at the end (9:17–19).[12] Each is

---

since the last two chapters are part of the canonical form of the book.

[10] I believe I owe this felicitous line to David Clines, but have not been able to locate it.

[11] See also the recent analysis of the discourse structure of Esther in the chart in Bush 1996: 301–304.

[12] Cf. Levenson 1997: 5–6. Levenson identifies ten banquets in Esther, which he groups into five sets of two. His table on p. 5, which indicates the structural relation-

connected with a significant reversal: Vashti and Esther, Haman and Mordecai, the Jews and their enemies. The contrasting motif of fasting appears near the middle of the book in chapter 4, and the two are brought together in chapter 9 in connection with Purim. The feasting of Purim is to be observed as the positive counterpoint to the fasting and lamentation prescribed for other times of the year (9:20–22, 31). Purim is a celebration of sorrow turned to joy, and mourning into celebration (9:22).

All this gives the central theme of deliverance a special character. It is *total* deliverance in the sense that it takes the form of a complete reversal, not only in the fortunes of the Jews themselves, but in their position in relation to their enemies. Levenson (1997: 8) has shown how the public humiliation of Haman in chapter 6 is the structural centre of the story, with the sequence of events before it being almost exactly reversed, item by item, in the sequence that follows. The way the plot is constructed emphasizes that Esther is a story not simply of rescue, but of reversal, of tables turned.

Our study of plot has already begun to put us in touch with the distinctive voice of the Esther story. Now we shall attempt to refine this by looking at some of the narrative's other defining qualities.

Special characteristics

Its strongly Jewish character

The term 'the Jews' (*hayyᵉhûḍîm*) springs into prominence in the Old Testament in connection with the demise of the kingdom of Judah (*yᵉhûḍâ*), and its eventual reconstitution as *yehud*, a province first of the Babylonian empire, and then of the Persian.[13] 'The Jews' becomes a standard term for people of Israelite descent who continue to look to *yehud* as their homeland, whether or not they live there. It occurs with varying frequency in the books of 2 Kings (once only), Jeremiah (nine times), Ezra (seven times), Nehemiah (eight times), Daniel (twice) and Esther (forty times). All these books are 'Jewish' in the sense that they have to do with the origins and characteristic way of life of 'the Jews' as a distinct people.[14]

But Esther is Jewish in a more heightened sense than this. Not only is the term used far more frequently than in other books, but the issue of

---

ships between the banquets, is adapted from a similar table by Fox.

[13] The more familiar designation 'Judea' springs from Greek and Roman times.

[14] So, of course, in an extended sense, is the entire OT.

Jewishness in an ethnic and religious sense is central to the plot. The deliverance it describes is of the Jewish people, and the festival that arises out of it is a Jewish festival. Its leading character is 'Mordecai the Jew', so designated six times (6:10; 8:7; 9:29, 31; 10:3; cf. 5:13).[15] Its chief villain is Haman, 'the enemy of the Jews', so called five times (3:10; 8:1; 9:10, 24; cf. 7:6). He harbours an ancient hostility towards Jews (3:1), and in the way he talks and behaves he is a classic anti-Semite. The theme of reversal turns centrally on the conflict between the Jews and their enemies, and its humour (of which more shortly) arises out of the way every attempt to destroy the Jews is foiled. This gives the Jewishness of the book an almost jingoistic quality. The survival of the Jews against all odds becomes virtually a principle of history. Mordecai believes in it (4:14), and so, apparently, does even Haman's wife (6:13). There is no more stridently Jewish book in the entire Old Testament.

Its Persian setting

The deliverance that takes place in Esther does so in a particular context and in a special set of circumstances. We have already noted how the distinctive ethos of the Persian court as presented in chapters 1 and 2 is critical for the way the main action develops. Now we consider the setting more generally.

As in the book of Nehemiah, the story begins in the royal city of Susa, at the heart of the vast Persian empire (Est. 1:2; cf. Neh. 1:1). Mordecai, like Nehemiah, is a loyal subject of the Persian emperor. Nehemiah's career begins approximately forty years later than Mordecai's,[16] and when we meet him he has already risen to high office. Mordecai is about to do so. But here the two works diverge sharply. The story of Nehemiah begins in Susa and ends in Jerusalem. It is a story of return. Mordecai and Esther's story runs its entire course in Persia. It is a story of Jews *living* in the eastern diaspora, and in Persia in particular. Persia is their entire and ever-present environment. The general problem they face is powerlessness. The particular problem is a policy of anti-Semitism instigated by someone who does have power.

---

[15] He is introduced as 'a Jewish man' ('*iš yᵉhûḏî*) in 2:5. Cf. Bush 1996: 312. Bush notes that 'this is the only time in the whole OT that a native member of the community of Israel is named and identified by a gentilic. Normally a member of the community of Israel is identified by a patronymic.'

[16] Assuming that the 'Artaxerxes' of Neh. 2:1 is Artaxerxes I, the successor of Xerxes (Ahasuerus), as is generally accepted. It is the date of Ezra's return, rather than Nehemiah's, that is problematical. See Bright 1972: 392–403.

A significant factor contributing to the deliverance that emerges in this setting is what we might call Mordecai's good citizenship. His reporting of the eunuchs' assassination plot (2:19–23) quite literally puts him in the king's good books and leads indirectly to his elevation to a position of authority, where he is able to thwart Haman's plans (6:1–11). Esther, too, rises to a place of influence partly through behaviour which wins her favour with the king (2:8–18).[17]

A little over a century earlier, Jeremiah had counselled the exiles of his day to engage positively with their foreign context (in Babylon) and not to listen to the hotheads among them who were urging them to do otherwise. 'This is what the LORD Almighty, the God of Israel, says ... seek the peace and prosperity of the city to which I have carried you into exile. Pray to the LORD for it, because if it prospers, you too will prosper' (Jer. 29:4–7). Here was the blueprint for an appropriate lifestyle for Jews in exile, the basic principle being a recognition of the interdependence of the Jewish community and its host environment.

W. L. Humphreys (1973) has argued that the express purpose of the original Esther story (which he thinks ended at ch. 8) was to commend such a lifestyle, and has pointed to an affinity in this respect between Esther 1 – 8 and the court tales of Daniel 1 – 6. The book as whole, however, (which is what we are concerned with here), can be said to commend such a lifestyle only incidentally. Its main purpose is to establish the proper observance of Purim. Nevertheless, the issue that Humphreys has highlighted remains a significant one. The story of Esther and Mordecai depicts characters responding to a particular life situation in a particular way. And the way their behaviour contributes to the outcome is an important aspect of how the plot works and of how the theme of deliverance is treated. The Persian setting is not just a neutral backdrop, but an active ingredient in the book's distinctive chemistry.

The portrayal of Mordecai and Esther as questionable heroes

Jeremiah's policy of constructive engagement was bound to be more difficult in practice than in theory, with hard questions developing along the interface between co-operation and capitulation. The book of Esther illustrates this in a striking way, with the behaviour of the leading characters hovering precariously between the commendable and the questionable.

---

[17] Though it is less obviously an instance of good citizenship. See further below.

Mordecai's reporting of the eunuchs' plot is a straightforward case of seeking the welfare of the king in a way that does not compromise his Jewishness. But what of his refusal to bow to Haman? No explicit judgment is passed on this by the author, but the story as told appears to provide two contrasting perspectives on it. Haman is an Agagite (3:1), and Mordecai is a descendant of Kish, the father of King Saul (2:5). Saul, we remember, was condemned by Samuel for failing to prosecute Yahweh's war against the Amalekites fully (1 Sam. 15:18; cf. Exod. 17:16), and for sparing Agag in particular (1 Sam. 15:20–33). Could Mordecai bow to such a man without denying his Jewishness?[18] Would it not be an act of craven capitulation and disloyalty to Yahweh? At the same time, however, to refuse to bow would be to flaunt his Jewishness in such a way as to expose all his fellow-Jews to danger. This issue is heightened by the fact that in the previous chapter we are told that Mordecai had warned Esther against doing this very thing (2:10).[19] To refuse to bow may have been heroic, but was it wise? Does Mordecai's refusal have the same character as the refusal of Daniel's three friends to bow to Nebuchadnezzar's golden image (Dan. 3), or is it an act of an entirely different order? There is no implication that Ahasuerus was requiring Haman to be worshipped as a god; simply that his rank be acknowledged in the customary Persian fashion.[20]

The same ambiguity attaches to Esther's actions. Her willingness to lay her life on the line for the sake of her people is noble indeed (4:16). But what of her unprotesting participation in the beauty competition, where she apparently succeeds by outperforming all her rivals in the king's bed (2:12–17)?

Here the contrasting episode involving Vashti is clearly of major significance (1:10–20). Vashti functions as a foil for Esther, but the precise implications of this are difficult to evaluate. Does Vashti's refusal set Esther's compliance in a positive light by illustrating that direct confrontation is counter-productive? Esther's subtle tactics, after all, do turn out to be far more successful than Vashti's provocative ones. But then Vashti must at the same time cast a negative light on the actions of Mordecai, whose refusal to bow appears as just another

[18] Cf. Bush (1996: 322), who notes that Moredecai's refusal to bow is portrayed as ethnic pride by the subtle use of patronymics. But he holds that the portrayal of Mordecai is consistently positive: 'the narrator takes for granted Mordecai's national pride and his faithfulness to ancient traditions and considers them wholly acceptable'.

[19] Contrast 2:10 with 3:4: 'He had told them that he was a Jew.'

[20] We know from Herodotus that bowing to superiors was a normal piece of Persian court etiquette, and even a regular way of acknowledging rank when Persians met one another in the street (*The Histories*: 96–97, 485). Cf. Gen. 27:29; 37:10; 41:43; 49:8.

instance of unwise confrontation. That it is subsequently overcome does not detract from the essentially negative character of the act itself.

It is possible, however, to see the function of the Vashti episode quite differently. Her stout refusal to be used by Ahasuerus has a heroic quality that we instinctively recognize, and this makes Esther's compliance, in what is in many ways a comparable situation, highly questionable. True, she was 'taken' into the palace (2:8). But could she not have refused, as Vashti had done? She would not thereby have endangered her fellow-Jews, since her own Jewishness was unknown at that time. True, subsequent events appear to vindicate her actions, but at what cost? Can she still be said to be a true Jew when she has sex with an uncircumcised pagan and feasts with him and Haman, in apparent disregard of Jewish dietary laws? Here the contrast with Daniel is striking, to say the least (Dan. 1:8).

There is no easy resolution of these matters, and we may simply be asking the wrong questions. It could be that the story emanates from circles with a very different view of what it means to be Jewish from that found elsewhere in the Old Testament. But the issues arise, in part at least, from within the story itself, and they inevitably assume a heightened significance when it is read as part of the Old Testament canon. Moreover, it is clear that the same questions troubled other readers before us. The Septuagint additions, which stem from the second century BC, include long, eloquent prayers by Mordecai and Esther in which they explain their actions.[21] Mordecai denies that his refusal to bow was motivated by pride, and Esther declares that she wears the royal crown only under duress, loathes the bed of the uncircumcised and takes no pleasure in the royal banquets.[22] These additions, among other things, turn the story into an exemplary tale in which the actions of the heroes are of unquestioned nobility and orthodoxy. But the very fact that such explanations were necessary shows that the canonical text itself is open to other interpretations. In short, in the book of Esther as it appears in the Masoretic Text, Esther and Mordecai do not have the same transparent goodness as a Daniel or a Joseph. Heroes they may be, but they are at best heroes of questionable morality and orthodoxy.

This means that the outcome cannot be seen simply as a reward. Could it perhaps be nothing more than good luck, or a simple case of

---

[21] See Baldwin 1984: 45–48, 119–126. For a more technical discussion, see Moore 1977: 153–168.

[22] The prayers of Mordecai and Esther both appear in Addition C, which follows 4:17 of the MT.

human courage and cleverness winning the day? The absence of any explicit reference to God would at first glance tend to point in this direction. But here too, things are not quite as simple as they seem.

The absence of any explicit reference to God

This absence is certainly one of the most striking features of the book. What clearly *is* present, however, is a whole series of remarkable coincidences which tip the balance of events in favour of the Jews at critical moments: the timely removal of Vashti, creating the opportunity for Esther to move into a position of power; Mordecai's equally fortuitous overhearing of the conspiratorial conversation of the eunuchs (2:21–22); the king's insomnia on the night before the proposed execution of Mordecai and his calling for the royal annals (6:1–2); the entry of Haman at the precise moment when the king is wondering how best to reward Mordecai (6:4); and the king's re-entry when Haman is compromising himself by falling on Esther's couch (7:8). All these incidents materially affect the outcome, but none is the result of any strategy on the part of the Jews. Either the Jews have extraordinarily good luck, or unseen powers are at work, giving events a particular shape and direction. The author never makes an explicit comment on this, one way or the other. However, the way the characters in the story behave, and the speeches they make at crucial points, clearly indicate *their* belief that something more than chance or purely natural causation is at work.

The casting of the *pûr* (the lot) by Haman and his friends at court at the beginning of the main action (3:7) implies a belief on their part that times such as particular days and months are not neutral. They have a tendency or bias towards certain outcomes, and it is not wise to make plans without consulting whatever powers give the times this special character. The lot is apparently a device for doing this.[23]

The three-day fast called by Mordecai at Esther's request in 4:15–16 is best understood in terms of a related, but significantly different, belief on the part of the Jews. It is quite distinct in character from the 'fasting, weeping and wailing' which are mentioned at the beginning of the same chapter (4:1–3). That was a spontaneous response to bad news. This fast, in contrast, is 'called' by Esther and Mordecai, and therefore takes on the character of a ritual act. Furthermore, it is

---

[23] Hallo (1983) describes a cube-shaped die in the Yale collection from ninth-century BC Assyria, with an inscription which twice uses the term *puru*, 'lot'. It illustrates how widespread was belief in predetermined fate. The die was used to determine the best time for all important events in the coming year. Cf. Baldwin 1984: 22–23.

specifically 'for' Esther (4:15), who is about to take her life in her hands by approaching the king unbidden; it has an intercessory aspect to it. The Jews apparently do not believe that particular events have a fixed character; but neither do they think that the way they turn out is entirely due to natural causes. The fasting here implies belief in a higher power who may be induced to intervene in a favourable way. The fast in question appears to be a religious act which it is hoped will induce him to do so on this particular occasion. But the outcome is not guaranteed by the act. There is no mechanical connection between ritual and result. The power who is appealed to remains free and sovereign: 'If I perish, I perish' (4:16). Against this background the passive expression of 9:22 acquires a particular nuance: 'sorrow *was turned for them* (*nehpak lāhem*) into joy, and mourning into a day of celebration' (my translation). In other words, their fasting met with a favourable response.

In this general connection two speeches, one by Mordecai and the other by Haman's wife and advisers, are of major significance. Both come at critical points in the plot. Mordecai's speech to Esther (in the form of a written message) comes directly before the calling of the three-day fast to which we have just referred, and in effect establishes the rationale for it:

> 'Do not think that because you are in the king's house you alone of all the Jews will escape. For if you remain silent at this time, relief and deliverance for the Jews will arise from another place, but you and your father's family will perish. And who knows but that you have come to royal position for such a time as this?' (4:12–14).

Mordecai expresses absolute certainty about two things. First, the Jews will survive. If Esther remains silent, relief and deliverance for them will come 'from another place'. The expression 'from another place' (*mimmāqôm 'aḥēr*) is tantalizingly vague. Mordecai does not know from where the help will come; only that its arrival is certain. The second thing of which he is certain is that Esther has a moral responsibility to act, and that if she declines to do so she will be punished: 'you and your father's family will perish'. This cannot mean that Esther and her family will be engulfed, along with their fellow Jews, in the general pogrom that is presently threatened. Mordecai is already certain that they will be saved from that. What is on view is a specific retribution that will be visited on Esther in some way as yet unknown. The final question of the speech raises the stakes even higher by lifting Esther's responsibility to act from a purely moral to a virtually religious level. It expresses a strong suspicion on Mordecai's part that Esther has been chosen for this very purpose: 'Who knows but that you may have come to royal position for such a time as this?'

In the rabbinic Judaism of later times the word 'place' (*māqôm*) became a circumlocution for 'God', a way of referring to him without naming him directly. Yahweh was 'the Place' *par excellence*. The term probably does not have that full technical sense here (cf. Fox 1991: 13–14), but it is certainly moving in that direction. It occurs in a context where there are strong implications of a higher power at work, shaping events towards a particular end. Within that framework, the responsibility of certain individuals to act in particular ways acquires a heightened significance. There are consequences, not just for others, but for the chosen ones themselves. There is a principle of retribution as well as deliverance in the divine workings, and it is a principle which cuts both ways. Even a Jew like Esther will not escape if she fails to comply with the divine will expressed in, among other things, the providential ordering of events.

We have already referred in passing to the speech by Haman's wife Zeresh and his advisers, literally his 'wise men' (6:13). It is made on Haman's return from parading Mordecai, his enemy, through the streets as 'the man the king delights to honour' (6:11). This speech is shorter than Mordecai's, and much more fatalistic in tone. If Mordecai is certain that the Jews will survive, Zeresh is equally certain that their enemies will be destroyed. There is no reference to any agent, human or divine; simply to an apparent law of history: 'If Mordecai, before whom you have begun to fall, is of Jewish descent, you cannot stand against him – you will surely come to ruin' (my translation). It is the most absolute statement in the whole book that history as a whole has a pro-Jewish shape to it, and it is surely ironic that it comes, not from the Jews themselves, but from their enemies.[24] It is the equivalent of the 'great fear' that falls on Israel's enemies in the conquest traditions,[25] something we shall see emerging again even more strongly as the book draws to a close (8:17). Zeresh here probably confronts Haman with something he himself already knows[26] but has been fighting against; this is a fight he cannot win.

---

[24] Mordecai and Esther at least have questions about short-term matters: 'who knows?' (4:14), and 'if I perish, I perish' (4:16). Zeresh has only certainty.

[25] Classically in Josh. 2:8–9.

[26] He has just told her and his friends 'everything that had happened to him' (6:13).

This brings us to the issue that lies at the very heart of this scroll's distinctiveness. Is it, or is it not, theological? Michael Fox thinks not. While the Esther story implies that 'There is a logic in history beyond natural causality', 'awareness of this logic does not lead to a particular theology' (1991: 246). Levenson's response to this, however, is incisive:

> This depends, of course, on what one defines as theology. If the definition requires explicit mention of God, then Fox wins the point. If, on the other hand, theology deals with the character of ultimate reality and its manifestation in human history, then Mordecai, Haman's advisers, and Zeresh have articulated the theology of the book of Esther rather completely: A hidden force arranges events in such a way that even against the most daunting odds the Jews are protected and delivered. The hiddenness of the force is an essential part of this theology (1997: 21).

Given the explicit link made between the Jews of the story, via Mordecai, and the exile of 'Jehoiachin king of Judah' in 2:6, there can be no question about the identity of this 'hidden force' from the author's point of view. It is Yahweh, the God of Israel. But he is never mentioned. Our concern here is not with why this is so (to which various answers have been given)[27] but with the effect of this remarkable feature of the story. How does the 'absence' of God colour the theme of deliverance in the book of Esther and contribute to its distinctive theology?

One thing it does is to set Esther off sharply from some deliverance narratives, such as the exodus from Egypt or the exploits of the judges, and align it closely with others, such as the stories of Joseph and Ruth. What these point to only partially, however, Esther carries to its logical conclusion. God is present even when he is most absent; when there are no miracles, dreams or visions, no charismatic leaders, no prophets to interpret what is happening, and not even any explicit God-talk. And he is present as deliverer. Those whom he saved by signs and wonders at the exodus he continues to save through his hidden, providential

---

Zeresh simply articulates what events show.

[27] The Mishnah holds that it is because Esther sanctions merrymaking that the name of God is omitted – so that it cannot inadvertently be profaned. Gordis (1981) has suggested that Esther is written in the style of a Persian chronicle composed by a Gentile scribe. The Jewish author indirectly testifies to his faith.

control of their history. His people are never simply at the mercy of blind fate or of malign powers, whether human or supernatural. Proverbs comes very close to distilling the theology of Esther in a single aphorism: 'The lot is cast into the lap, but its decision is wholly from Yahweh' (Prov. 16:33, my translation). But, as Baldwin notes, Esther goes even further than this: 'even when the dice had fallen the Lord was powerful to reverse its good omen into bad, in order to deliver his people' (1984: 23).

Its humour

We have already touched on this, and shall return to it again as we draw this chapter to a close. A brief comment must suffice at this point.

Despite the seriousness of the crisis with which it deals, the book evokes laughter at many points. The scene involving Vashti, for example, makes Ahasuerus look very foolish indeed. He who rules over 127 provinces cannot rule his own wife. The sight of the king treating his insomnia with a dose of reading from the royal annals is softly satirical, as is his confusion when he is caught in the crossfire between Esther and his prime minister. It takes him more than half the story to work out who is his friend and who is his enemy. But the most savage humour is at Haman's expense, especially in chapter 6. The spectacle of the villain hoist on his own petard is one that the author clearly enjoys, and expects us to enjoy also. The ironic reversals Yahweh brings about in order to confound the enemies of his people are a cause for hilarious celebration. And that note of celebration is realized in the humour of the story itself before it is institutionalized in the festivities of Purim. The laughter the story evokes is part of its distinctiveness, and an important aspect of the message it delivers.

Such, then, is the book of Esther. Its purpose is to establish the proper observance of Purim. But its theme is deliverance, deliverance that emerges in the midst of life with its apparently normal flux of events. It is about a world in which Gentiles hold power, and Jews must watch their every step; a world which throws up hard ethical and religious questions, and where very imperfect people struggle to respond responsibly to events they do not fully understand and certainly do not control. It is about fasting and feasting, tears and laughter, in a world where God is present, even when he seems absent. But how does it relate to its wider Old Testament context? It is to this issue that we now turn.

II

The way Esther related to the rest of the Hebrew Scriptures was a question that troubled Jewish thinkers for at least the first three centuries of the Christian era. Some argued that it did not really belong in the canon at all, since it promoted a festival not endorsed by the Torah. Others, with an eye to the continuing tense relations between Jews and Gentiles, were concerned at its apparently vindictive spirit.[28] But the popularity of Purim among the Jews had made the canonicity of Esther virtually a *fait accompli* as early as the second century BC.[29] The real issue that remained was not whether it was canonical, but how to harmonize it with the rest of the Jewish Scriptures. The answer was found in Exodus 17:14: 'Write this as a memorial in a book, and rehearse it in the ears of Joshua, for I will utterly blot out the name of Amalek from under heaven' (my translation). This was taken as divine authorization, given in advance, for the writing of Esther and therefore its reception as Scripture.[30]

Our concern here is not with the canonicity of Esther as such, but with how it functions in its context, how it contributes to what the whole of the Old Testament is about. The way the rabbis related it to its context was driven by their particular apologetic concerns. However, it does highlight an issue which is of first importance for us also: namely, that the story of Esther and Mordecai is indissolubly bound into salvation history as the entire Old Testament presents it.

The fall of Jerusalem in the sixth century BC was a crucial moment in this history. It was the fact of exile that posed most acutely the issues of Jewish identity and the survival of Israel. An explicit link is made with this event, as we have seen, in 2:6. Mordecai, like Ezekiel, is identified as one whose situation is traceable back to Nebuchadnezzar's deportation of Jehoiachin and other leading citizens of Jerusalem in 597 BC (cf. Ezek. 1:2). Furthermore, the rabbis were right to see a connection between Esther and Exodus 17, though they did not explore its full theological implications. Given the reference to Mordecai as a 'son of Kish' in 2:5, the identification of Haman as 'the Agagite' in 3:1 is a transparent allusion to the confrontation between Saul, son of Kish,

---

[28] TB *Megilloth* 7a.

[29] Cf. Beckwith 1985: 312. Esther was probably added to the canon about 164 BC, in the aftermath of the Maccabean revolt. The Greek additions preserved in the LXX begin the process of harmonizing it with the rest of Scripture.

[30] TJ *Megilloth* 70d. It was asserted that Esther was dictated to Moses on Mount Sinai and finally committed to writing in the time of Mordecai. Cf. Anderson 1950: 32–33.

and Agag the Amalekite in 1 Samuel 15. But this is expressly linked in the first two verses of that chapter to the incident recorded in Exodus 17, which culminates in the declaration by Moses, 'Yahweh will be at war with Amalek from generation to generation' (v. 16, my translation). Through Mordecai and Esther, Yahweh continues the war with Amalek he began with Moses. Mordecai's refusal to bow is simply the trigger that opens the next chapter in the conflict. This is the theological explanation for the holy-war motifs that appear in Esther, including the fear that seizes the enemy (8:17).[31]

We cannot stop here, however, for in the larger framework of salvation history the war against Amalek has a particular covenantal significance. It begins when the Amalekites try to destroy Israel after their exodus from Egypt (Exod. 17:8). But in the book of Exodus the deliverance from Egypt has already been linked to the promises made to the patriarchs: 'God heard their groaning, and he remembered his covenant with Abraham, Isaac and Jacob' (Exod. 2:24). Against this background, the war with Amalek, which goes on from generation to generation through the Old Testament, is a particular manifestation in history of Yahweh's covenant promise to be Israel's defence against her enemies: 'I will make you into a great nation ... I will bless those who bless you, *and whoever curses you I will curse*' (Gen. 12:2–3, my italics).

Eugene Peterson has also noted a more subtle way in which the Esther story relates to Abraham. The setting in Susa puts it at the far edge of biblical history, both geographically and chronologically. It was close to here, not far from Susa, that the whole story of salvation began:

One hundred and fifty miles southwest of Susa and fourteen hundred years earlier, Abraham had set out from Ur and travelled westward, following the arc of the fertile crescent, all the way to Egypt. He personally paced off nearly the whole territory on which the biblical story would be lived out over the next two thousand years. God's call to Abraham began with a promise that he would be the founder of a community of faith (1992: 203).

---

[31] The way the plunder is treated may also reflect the requirements of holy war (cf. Josh. 7:1; etc), although here the details of the story cut both ways. The king's edict of 8:11, which was drafted by Mordecai (8:9), permits plundering of the enemies' goods, but 9:10 insists that this was not in fact done.

Actually, Abraham was promised much more than this: a land, a great name, protection, and that his descendants would become a blessing to all peoples of the earth (Gen. 12:1–3).

In the book of Esther, salvation history has come full circle, back to the edge again. There seems just as little prospect of the promises being fulfilled at the end as there was at the beginning. Perhaps even less. Given the absence of explicitly religious language, 'a community of faith' seems too strong for what we have in Esther. The Jews in Susa are not shining examples of what it means to be children of Abraham. But they are Jews, and therefore his children none the less. They exist, and they are a community; and in its own inimitable way the story testifies to the fact that the promises are not at an end, even here. For if this community is at the edge, it is also at the centre. Susa was the administrative centre of a vast empire that spanned all the land once traversed by Abraham, including Palestine. And when a plan is hatched to annihilate his descendants throughout all of its 127 provinces, Esther and Mordecai are providentially in a position to prevent it.

It is in this context that the deliverance theme of the book is finally to be understood. It is not the same kind of deliverance that Israel experienced at the exodus. That was achieved by the manifest, powerful, miraculous intervention of God; this one is accomplished by his providential overruling of natural events. But Passover and Purim, standing back to back in the festival cycle, testify to two complementary aspects of a single reality: the election of Israel, which had its beginning historically in the call of Abraham. We have lingered over this point because of its crucial hermeneutical significance. Recognizing that Esther is part of the history of salvation in the Old Testament is basic to appreciating its relationship to the continuing history of salvation in the New. We are now in a position to address this issue directly.

III

On the whole, the Christian church had very little to say about Esther in the first 400 years of its history.[32] It is likely that the book was always accepted as canonical in the West, although it is referred to only by Clement of Rome (in the first century; *1 Clem.* 55) and Hippolytus (in the third), neither of whom indicates whether or not he regarded it as

---

[32] The material in the rest of this paragraph is essentially a summary of the detailed review of the subject by Beckwith (1985: 296–308).

Scripture. In the East, opinion appears to have been divided, with some following Miletus, who excluded it from his list of canonical books, and others following Origen, who put it in.[33] Only Clement of Alexandria, in the late third century, provides us with any indication of how Christians who did regard it as Scripture managed to appropriate it as such. He says that Esther clothed herself 'mystically', as a type of redemption (*Paedagogue* 3.12.5). It was not until the late fourth century, however, at the Council of Carthage (AD 397), that Esther was formally accorded a secure place in the Christian Scriptures, and then only with the pious amplifications it had been given in the Septuagint.

We may justifiably detect, behind all this, a certain awkwardness that the Christian church has felt in appropriating Esther as part of its own canon. Even the Reformed tradition, which has generally been strongly committed to the exposition of Scripture, including the Old Testament, as the Word of God, has not had the happiest of relationships with Esther. As far as we know, Calvin never preached from it. Luther not only ignored it, but pronounced against it in characteristically vigorous terms. In his famous saying on the subject, he lumped Esther and 2 Maccabees together: 'I am so hostile to the book [2 Maccabees] and to Esther, that I wish they did not exist at all; for they Judaize too much, and are full of heathen perverseness' (*Table Talk*, Weimar Ausgabe 22.2080). Despite this, Protestants have continued to recognize Esther as canonical, and without the Septuagint additions (cf. Larkin 1996: 63).

By rejecting those additions, the Reformers and those who followed them effectively blocked the way to any appropriation of Esther which involved moralizing. As we have seen, it was these additions that began the moralizing tradition by giving Esther the character of an exemplary tale. But this was not true to its real character. The Esther of the Hebrew canon has, as Luther put it, much 'heathen perverseness' in it. And the real difficulty for the moralist, Jewish or Christian, is that the perverseness is not all on the side of the villains. We have noted the questionable character of the actions of Esther and Mordecai, even when they are being heroic. And when they finally have the power to do so, they act with a vindictiveness and cruelty that are not far removed from those of Haman himself. It is to Luther's credit that he did not try to appropriate Esther by moralizing.

Nor does the mystical-typological approach of Clement of Alexandria offer a viable alternative. This takes elements from the story, such as Esther putting on her royal robes (5:1), and attaches Christian meanings

---

[33] In his commentary on Pss. 1 – 25.

to them without any reference to the way they function in the story itself. The plain sense of the text is ignored in the interests of a 'quick fix' approach to Christian appropriation. The Reformers were right not to adopt this way of reading Esther either.

But this leaves us with Luther's most serious objection to Esther: its strident Jewishness. Luther's stricture that 'it Judaizes too much' was, I presume, a direct outcome of his commitment to reading it in its plain, historical sense, and therefore requires a careful response from us.

It has become fashionable in recent years to use the Jewishness of Esther as the platform for a kind of reverse moralizing. On this view, what Luther objected to is precisely what makes Esther an invaluable part of the Christian Bible. Its role is to confront us continually with God's commitment to the survival of Israel in an ethnic sense, and to warn Christians against the evils of anti-Semitism.[34] We must find ourselves in the story, not in the Jewish heroes, Esther and Mordecai, but in the Gentile villains, Haman and Ahasuerus. The laughter of the story is at our expense as much as theirs, and we must be big enough to take it on the chin, recognizing that it is thoroughly deserved and is good for us.

Now there is clearly some truth in this. The history of the church is too stained with anti-Semitism to allow us to think we do not need to be rebuked for it or warned against it. Furthermore, it may well be an incidental function of Esther to do this as part of the canon. But to make this its main function is to overturn the whole structure of the Bible's theology. For the New Testament consistently encourages Christians to make the stories of God's dealings with Israel under the old covenant part of their own story, and to see themselves, not in the Pharaohs, Nebuchadnezzars and Hamans of the Old Testament, but in Abraham, Moses, Elijah, Job, and so on. In other words the promise–fulfilment relationship between the Testaments, which is implied by the gospel itself, not only makes it legitimate for Christians to read Esther as part of their own story, but actually requires them to do so. This is not to 'spiritualise the concept of Israel', as Childs (1979: 606) has put it, but to recognize that from the perspective of the New Testament the election of Israel in Abraham had a purpose which is realized in Christ and the gospel (see especially Gal. 3:15–22).

At the heart of the book of Esther lies a conflict between two communities. When Haman speaks of 'a certain people dispersed and scattered among the peoples ... whose customs are different from those of all other people' (3:8), he identifies the basic problem, the tinder that

---

[34] So e.g. Fox (1991), Bos (1986), and (by implication) Childs (1979).

needs only a spark to ignite it. The Jews are different. Their law, in particular, is a barrier that separates them from others and arouses suspicion and resentment.

Under the new covenant this 'dividing wall of hostility ... the law with its commandments and regulations' is done away with by the cross, and believing Jews and Gentiles are constituted one new people in Christ (Eph. 2:11–22). Outside of this, attempts to solve the problem of the conflict between Jew and Gentile continue, with mixed results. But the God-given solution is found in the gospel.[35]

What is significant for us here, however, is that, even under the new covenant, the scandal of particularity remains. There is still an elect people, and there are those who hate them. The elect are no longer defined by their adherence to the law, but by their identification with Christ (Matt. 5:11). They are the elect strangers of the dispersion, with an obligation to honour those who rule over them as far as is consistent with their loyalty to Christ (1 Pet. 1:1; 2:13–17). This analogy of context to which the New Testament consistently bears witness enables the book of Esther to speak powerfully to Christians without being false to itself. In fact, of all the narratives of the Old Testament, it is precisely those that deal with the people of God in exile (the stories of Joseph, Daniel and Esther) that resonate most strongly with the circumstances of the new-covenant people of God.

In particular, the hiddenness of God that we find in Esther mirrors the world many of us live in today, particularly in the West. Events seem to take their normal course, and miracles are few and far between, if they occur at all. But if we have read Esther correctly, it testifies in a striking way to the fact that the absence of the miraculous does not mean the absence of God. He remains committed to the welfare of his people, and works all things for their good, even when he is most hidden. This message about the special providence of God is one that is reiterated in the New Testament and one that God's people still – and perhaps especially – need to hear today (Rom. 8:28).

The humorous quality of the story, too, must enter into our appropriation of it. There is no obligation for Christians to celebrate

---

[35] This matter was addressed during and soon after the Second World War with its anti-Semitic horrors in two important works to which my own thinking is much indebted: Vischer 1937 and Anderson 1950. Anderson strongly criticizes Vischer's typological treatment of details of the Esther story, but endorses his basic contention that 'the Jewish question ... is "die Gottesfrage", i.e. the problem posed by God in the election of Israel', and that 'Whoever eliminates the book of Esther from the Bible ... says herewith: the Jewish question and its solution have nothing to do with the revelation of God in Jesus Christ' (1950: 36–37).

Purim, any more than to observe any other rite of the old covenant. But, as part of their Bible, the book of Esther continues to evoke laughter which is not to be denigrated in the interests of a higher Christian morality.[36] Although the humour of the story is tainted at times with vindictiveness, the way Purim is instituted in the last chapter of the book seems deliberately intended to purge it of this and to bring out its true character as the laughter of pure astonishment at a deliverance that came about unexpectedly, like a gift – 'days of feasting and joy and giving presents of food to one another and gifts to the poor' (9:22). Seen in this light, the laughter of the book of Esther is like that of Psalm 126:1–3:

> When the LORD brought back the captives to Zion,
>   we were like men who dreamed.
> Our mouths were filled with laughter,
>   our tongues with songs of joy.
> Then it was said among the nations,
>   'The LORD has done great things for them.'
> The LORD has done great things for us,
>   and we are filled with joy.

There may be incidental, salutary lessons that we can learn by identifying with Haman,[37] but essentially what the story invites us to do is not to identify with him, but to rejoice at his downfall. Haman is not us, but our enemy. He embodies, in a most striking way, that inveterate hatred that the world has always had, and always will have, for God's people (John 17:14). And his downfall is not our achievement, but God's – a gift to be marvelled at and rejoiced in. As part of its total message, the Bible's laughter is an anticipation of the eschaton; a reminder of the fact that, in a world where God remains sovereign, it is not the proud and cruel who will have the last laugh, but God and his people (Rev. 18:20).

The book of Esther is indeed a festive garment, a garment to put on when we are astonished, once again, at some unexpected way God has rescued us, and when we are ready to celebrate. But it is also a garment to put on when the forces arrayed against us seem all-powerful, when to

---

[36] As Anderson does, by implication: 'It is significant that the Book of Esther is never once quoted in the New Testament, despite its popularity among the Jews of the first century ... If a Christian minister is faithful to the context, he will not take his text from Esther ... Jesus Christ both unites inseparably and at the same time draws the sharpest cleavage between the Old and New Covenants' (1950: 42).

[37] E.g the self-destructive character of pride, lust for power, and racism.

laugh may be the only way to stay sane. To put this garment on, however, is not to whistle in the dark, or to pretend that things are other than they are. It is to clothe ourselves with the truth that God is sovereign, and to be reminded that he is always with us, even when he seems most absent, and that nothing can ultimately thwart his purposes. To put on Esther is to affirm that God is our deliverer, and to share in the laughter of heaven.

Epilogue

The Five Scrolls that we have studied in this volume constitute something of a frontier in biblical studies. Three of them have had questions raised about their inspiration and authority, and there has been uncertainty about where the other two belong (in the Prophets or Writings) and how they should be regarded (as works in their own right or as supplements to other books). All of them are marginal in one way or another: they hover at the edge of the canon.

They also represent a frontier theologically. God is not mentioned at all in one of them. Another contains only one oblique reference to him, and they all pose some unnerving, radical questions that come in from left field, as it were, and force us to go back and think again about matters we may have begun to take for granted.[1] We have seen how Ecclesiastes, for example, forces us to think again about Proverbs. The Song of Songs demands that we reflect again on Genesis 1 – 3. Ruth makes us go back and think again about the Torah; what does it really mean to keep the law of Moses? And so we could go on. The raising of such questions is perhaps the special contribution of 'problem' books such as these. Like the prods of a shepherd, they stop us from wandering from the pathway of wisdom through mental laziness (cf. Eccles. 12:11).

To put it slightly differently, we might say that these scrolls pose crucial questions about the centre and coherence of the Bible's theology by exploring its boundaries. They raise questions about the unity of the Bible, and about how the Old Testament in particular can be the word of God for us today. All of them are test cases, I believe, of the viability of biblical theology, and of its value as a key to the proper reading of the Old Testament as part of the Christian Bible.

---

[1] They are also among the books most ignored by the NT writers. Carr (1981: 99) notes that 'All the OT books except Ruth, Ezra, Ecclesiastes and Song of Solomon are quoted [in the NT].' There are important connections, as we have seen, between the genealogies of Ruth 4 and Matt. 1, but whether or not this could be considered quotation is open to question.

In this book, we have been doing some boundary-riding in biblical theology. I have found it taxing (these books are challenging), but also exhilarating, and I trust it has been the same for you. Above all, I hope that you have met God in the process, and have come back convinced that all Scripture bears his imprint, and determined to go on exploring its riches yourself and sharing them with others.

Bibliography

Aland, K., et al, (eds.) (1983). *The Greek New Testament*. Third edition (corrected). London: United Bible Societies.

Albrektson, B. (1963). *Studies in the Text and Theology of the Book of Lamentations*. Lund: Gleerup.

Alter, R. (1981). *The Art of Biblical Narrative*. New York: Basic Books.

Anderson, B. W. (1950). 'The place of the book of Esther in the Christian Bible'. *Journal of Religion* 30: 32–43.

Bailey, K. E. (1991). 'The fall of Jerusalem and St Mark's account of the cross'. *Expository Times* 102.4: 102–105.

Baldwin, J. G. (1984). *Esther: An Introduction and Commentary*. Tyndale Old Testament Commentaries. Leicester and Downers Grove, IL: IVP.

Barker, P. A. (1998). 'The theology of Deuteronomy 27'. *Tyndale Bulletin* 49.2: 277–304.

Barr, J. (1999). *The Concept of Biblical Theology: An Old Testament Perspective*. London: SCM.

Barth, Karl (1960). *Church Dogmatics 3: The Doctrine of Creation*, Part Two. Edinburgh: T. and T. Clark.

Beattie, D. R. G. (1977). *Jewish Exegesis of the Book of Ruth*. Sheffield: JSOT Press.

Beckwith, R. (1985). *The Old Testament Canon of the New Testament Church and its Background in Early Judaism*. London: SPCK.

Bertman, S. (1965). 'Symmetrical design in the book of Ruth'. *Journal of Biblical Literature* 84: 165–168.

Bos, J. W. H. (1986). *Ruth, Esther, Jonah*. Knox Preaching Guides. Atlanta: John Knox.

Bright, J. (1972). *A History of Israel*. Second edition. London: SCM.

Brown, W. P. (1996). *Character in Crisis: A Fresh Approach to the Wisdom Literature of the Old Testament*. Grand Rapids: Eerdmans.

Bush, F. W. (1996). *Ruth, Esther*. Word Biblical Commentary. Dallas: Word.

Campbell, E. F. (1972). *Ruth: A New Translation with Introduction and Commentary*. The Anchor Bible. New York: Doubleday.

Carr, G. L. (1981). 'The Old Testament love songs and their use in the New Testament'. *Journal of the Evangelical Theological Society* 24.2: 97–105.

————(1984). *The Song of Solomon: An Introduction and Commentary.* Tyndale Old Testament Commentaries. Leicester and Downers Grove, IL: IVP.

————(1993). 'Song of Songs', in L. Ryken & T. Longman III (eds.), *A Complete Literary Guide to the Bible*: 281–295. Grand Rapids: Zondervan.

Carson, D. A. (1995). 'Current issues in biblical theology: a New Testament perspective'. *Bulletin for Biblical Research* 5: 17–41.

Castellino, A. B. (1968). 'Qohelet and his Wisdom'. *Catholic Biblical Quarterly* 30.1: 15–28.

Charry, E. T. (1987). 'Female sexuality as an image of empowerment: two models'. *Saint Luke's Journal of Theology* 30.3: 201–218.

Childs, B. S. (1979). 'Esther', in *Introduction to the Old Testament as Scripture*: ch. 40. London: SCM.

Clines, D. J. A. (1984). *The Esther Scroll: The Story of the Story. Journal for the Study of the Old Testament* Supplement Series 30. Sheffield: JSOT Press.

————(1991). 'In quest of the historical Mordecai'. *Vetus Testamentum* 41.2: 129–136.

Crenshaw, J. L. (1987). *Ecclesiastes: A Commentary.* Old Testament Library. Philadelphia: Westminster.

Dempster, S. (1997). 'An "extraordinary fact": Torah and temple and the contours of the Hebrew canon, Part 1'. *Tyndale Bulletin* 48.1: 23–56.

Dumbrell, W. J. (1988). 'Lamentations', in *The Faith of Israel: Its Expression in the Books of the Old Testament*: ch. 31. Leicester: Apollos.

Ellul, J. (1990). *Reason for Being: A Meditation on Ecclesiastes.* Grand Rapids: Eerdmans.

Falk, M. (1982). *Love Lyrics from the Bible: A Translation and Literary Study of The Song of Songs.* Sheffield: Almond.

Fewell, D. N., & Gunn, D. M. (1990). *Compromising Redemption: Relating Characters in the Book of Ruth.* Louisville, KY: Westminster/John Knox.

Fleming, D. C. (1982). *Job, Proverbs, Ecclesiastes, Song of Solomon.* The Old Testament Speaks 6. Hong Kong: Living Books for All.

Forman, C. C. (1956). 'Koheleth's use of Genesis'. *Journal of Semitic Studies* 5: 262.

Fox, M. V. (1977). 'Frame-narrative and composition in the book of Qoheleth'. *Hebrew Union College Annual* 48: 83–106.

————(1991). *Character and Ideology in the Book of Esther.* Carolina: University of South Carolina Press.

Fredericks, D. C. (1993). *Coping with Transcience: Ecclesiastes on Brevity in Life.* The Biblical Seminar 18. Sheffield: Sheffield Academic Press.

Freeman, D. (1996), 'Pentecost, Feast of', in I. H. Marshall et al. (eds.), *New Bible Dictionary*: 898–899. Third edition. Leicester and Downers Grove, IL: IVP.

Gabler, J. P. (1787). 'An oration on the proper distinction between biblical and dogmatic theology and the specific objectives of each', in B. C. Oltenburger, E. A. Martens & G. F. Hasel (eds.) (1992), *The Flowering of Old Testament Theology: A Reader in Twentieth-Century Old Testament Theology, 1930–1990*: 492–502. Winona Lake: Eisenbrauns.

Gibson, R. J. (ed.) (1997). *Interpreting God's Plan: Biblical Theology and the Pastor.* Explorations 11. Carlisle: Paternoster; Adelaide: Open Book.

Ginsberg, H. L. (1960). 'The structure and contents of the book of Ecclesiastes', in M. Noth & D. Winton Thomas (eds.), *Wisdom in Israel and the Ancient Near East.* Supplements to *Vetus Testamentum* 3: 138–149. Leiden: Brill.

Goldsworthy, G. L. (1997). 'Is biblical theology viable?', in Gibson (ed.) (1997): 18–46.

Gordis, R. (1974). *The Song of Songs and Lamentations: A Study, Modern Translation and Commentary.* New York: KTAV.

————(1981). 'Religion, wisdom and history in the book of Esther – a new solution to an ancient crux'. *Journal of Biblical Literature* 100.3: 359–388.

Gottwald, N. K. (1962). *Studies in the Book of Lamentations.* Studies in Biblical Theology 14. Revised edition. London: SCM.

Hallo, W. W. (1983). 'The first Purim'. *Biblical Archaeologist* 46.1: 19–28.

Herodotus. *The Histories.* Revised edition. A. de Selincourt (trans.) Middlesex: Penguin, 1972.

Herzog, A. (1971). 'Musical rendition. the Song of Songs, Ruth, and Ecclesiastes', in C. Roth, G. Wigoder et al. (eds.), *Encyclopaedia Judaica* 14, *RED–SL*: 1058–1059. Jerusalem: Keter.

Hillers, D. B. (1992). *Lamentations: A New Translation, with Introduction and Commentary.* The Anchor Bible. Second, revised edition. New York: Doubleday.

Holmgren, F. C. (1999). *The Old Testament and the Significance of Jesus: Embracing Change – Maintaining Christian Identity: The Emerging Center in Biblical Scholarship.* Grand Rapids: Eerdmans.

Hubbard, R. L., Jr (1988). *The Book of Ruth.* New International Commentary on the Old Testament. Grand Rapids: Eerdmans.

Humphreys, W. L. (1973). 'A lifestyle for diaspora: a study of the tales of Esther and Daniel'. *Journal of Biblical Literature* 92: 211–223.

de Jong, S. (1992). 'A book on labour: the structuring principles and the main theme of the book of Qohelet'. *Journal for the Study of the Old Testament* 54: 107–116.

Josephus, *Against Apion.* In W. Whiston (trans.) (1987), *The Works of Josephus, Complete and Unabridged.* New updated edition. Massachusetts: Hendrickson.

————*The Antiquities of the Jews.* In W. Whiston (trans.) (1987), *The Works of Josephus, Complete and Unabridged.* New updated edition. Massachusetts: Hendrickson.

Kaiser, W. C., Jr. (1979). *Ecclesiastes: Total Life.* Everyman's Bible Commentary. Chicago: Moody.

Kidner, D. (1985). *Wisdom to Live By: An Introduction to the Old Testament Wisdom Books of Proverbs, Job and Ecclesiastes.* Leicester: IVP.

Landy, F. (1979). 'The Song of Songs and the Garden of Eden'. *Journal of Biblical Literature* 98: 513–528.

Larkin, K. J. A. (1996). *Ruth and Esther.* Old Testament Guides. Sheffield: JSOT Press.

Levenson, J. D. (1997). *Esther.* Old Testament Library. Louisville, KY: Westminster/John Knox.

Loader, J. A. (1979). *Polar Structures in the Book of Qohelet.* Beihefte zur *Zeitschrift für die alttestamentliche Wissenschaft* 152. Berlin: de Gruyter.

Loewe, R. (1966). 'Apologetic motifs in the targum to the Song of Songs', in A. Altmann (ed.), *Biblical Motifs: Origins and Transformations*: 159–196. London: Oxford University Press.

Longman, Tremper, III (1998). *The Book of Ecclesiastes.* New International Commentary on the Old Testament. Grand Rapids: Eerdmans.

Lys, D. (1968). *Le plus beau chant de la création: Commentaire du Cantique des Cantiques.* Lectio Divina, 51. Paris: Cerf.

MacDonald, D. B. (1933). *The Hebrew Literary Genius: An Interpretation, being an Introduction to the Reading of the Old*

Testament. Princeton: Princeton University Press.

Moore, C. A. (1977). *Daniel, Esther and Jeremiah: The Additions*. The Anchor Bible. New York: Doubleday.

Murphy, R. (1992). *Ecclesiastes*. Word Biblical Commentary. Dallas: Word.

Ortlund, R. C., Jr (1996). *Whoredom: God's Unfaithful Wife in Biblical Theology*. New Studies in Biblical Theology 2. Leicester: Apollos; Grand Rapids: Eerdmans.

Peterson, E. H. (1992). *Five Smooth Stones for Pastoral Work.* Grand Rapids: Eerdmans.

Pope, M. H. (1977). *The Song of Songs: A New Translation with Introduction and Commentary*. The Anchor Bible. New York: Doubleday.

Pritchard, J. B. (ed.) (1969). *Ancient Near Eastern Texts Relating to the Old Testament.* Third edition with supplement. Princeton: Princeton University Press.

Rauber, D. F. (1970). 'Literary values in the Bible: Ruth'. *Journal of Biblical Literature* 89: 27–37.

Richardson, J. (1995). *God, Sex and Marriage: Guidance from 1 Corinthians 7*. London: MPA Books.

Robinson, D. W. B. (1997). 'Origins and unresolved tensions', in Gibson (ed.) (1970): 1–17.

Roth, C., et al. (1971). 'Scrolls, The Five'. In C. Roth, G. Wigoder, et al. (eds.), *Encyclopaedia Judaica* 14, *RED–SL*: 1057–1058. Jerusalem: Keter.

Rowley, H. H. (1965). 'The marriage of Ruth', in *The Servant of the Lord and Other Essays*: ch. 5. Oxford: Blackwell.

Ryken, L. (1979). *Triumphs of the Imagination: Literature in Christian Perspective*. Downers Grove, IL, and Leicester: IVP.

Sailhamer, J. H. (1991). 'The Mosaic law and the theology of the Pentateuch'. *Westminster Theological Journal* 53: 24–61.

Seow, C. L. (1992). 'The farce of the wise king: rhetoric and subversion in Qohelet 1:12 – 2:11'. A paper read at the Society of Biblical Literature meeting, San Franscisco.

Shelley, P. B. (1943). *The Complete Poetical Works of Percy Bysshe Shelley.* T. Hutchinson (ed.). London: Oxford University Press.

Trible, P. (1973). 'Depatriarchalizing in biblical interpretation'. *Journal of the American Academy of Religion* 41: 30–48.

————(1978). *God and the Rhetoric of Sexuality*. Philadelphia: Fortress.

Vanhoozer, K. J. (forthcoming). 'Exegesis and hermeneutics', in *New*

Dictionary of Biblical Theology. Leicester: IVP.

Vischer, W. (1937). *Esther*. Theologische Existenz heute 48. Munich: Kaiser.

Webb, B. G. (1994). 'Homosexuality in Scripture', in B. G. Webb (ed.), *Theological and Pastoral Responses to Homosexuality*. Explorations 8: 65–104. Adelaide: Open Book.

————(1997). 'Biblical theology and biblical interpretation', in Gibson (ed.) (1997): 47–74.

Wright, A. G. (1976). 'The riddle of the Sphinx: the structure of the book of Qoheleth', in J. L. Crenshaw (ed.), *Studies in Ancient Israelite Wisdom*. New York: KTAV.

Index of modern authors

Aland, K., 79
Albrektson, B., 76–77
Alter, R., 114
Anderson, B. W., 126, 131–132

Bailey, K. E., 80–81
Baldwin, J. G., 120–121, 125
Barker, P. A., 76
Barr, J., 15
Barth, K., 30
Beattie, D. R. G., 47–48
Beckwith, R., 13, 28, 106, 126, 128
Bertman, S., 38
Bos, J. W. H., 130
Bright, J., 117
Brown, W. P., 93, 105, 106
Bush, F. W., 114–115, 117

Calvin, J., 129
Campbell, E. F., 52–53
Carr, G. L., 17, 22–23, 135
Carson, D. A., 15
Castellino, A. B., 85–86
Charry, E. T., 31
Childs, B. S., 130
Clines, D. J. A., 112, 114–115
Crenshaw, J. L., 92

Delitzsch, F., 84
Dempster, S., 76
Dumbrell, W. J. D., 78

Ellul, J., 104

Falk, M., 19–22
Fewell, D. N., 43
Fleming, D. C., 26
Forman, C. C., 104

Fox, M. V., 101–102, 111–113, 115, 123–124, 130
Fredericks, D. C., 100
Freeman, D., 55

Gabler, J. P., 14–15
Gibson, R. J., 15
Ginsberg, H. L., 85
Goldsworthy, G. L., 15
Gordis, R., 32, 124
Gottwald, N. K., 62, 68, 72, 76–77
Gunn, D. M., 43

Hallo, W. W., 121
Hillers, D. B., 61–62, 66, 76
Holmgren, F. C., 106
Hubbard, R. L., Jr, 38
Humphreys, W. L., 118

de Jong, S., 86–89, 96–98

Kaiser, W. C., 85
Kidner, D., 107

Landy, F., 23, 28, 31
Larkin, K. J. A., 37, 40–42, 51, 129
Lawhead, S., 59
Levenson, J. D., 112, 116, 124
Loader, J. A., 87
Loewe, R., 28
Longman, T., III, 102
Luther, M., 129–130
Lys, D., 30

MacDonald, D. B., 104
Marvell, A., 21
Moore, C. A., 120

Murphy, R., 92, 101

Ortlund, R. C., Jr, 34

Peterson, E., 28–29, 69, 71, 74, 90, 111, 127
Pope, M. H., 18, 23, 29

Rauber, D. F., 45, 50, 53
Richardson, J., 34
Robinson, D. W. B., 15
Roth, C., 106, 111
Rowley, H. H., 54
Ryken, L., 114

Sailhamer, J. H., 76
Sayer, D. A., 17
Seow, C.-L., 93
Shelley, P. B., 93
Trible, P., 31

Vanhoozer, K. J., 15
Vischer, W., 131

Webb, B. G., 16, 32
Wright, A. G., 85–86

Index of Scripture references

Genesis
1:1–31 33, 103
1:1 – 2:25 32
1:1 – 3:24 30, 33,
  103, 135
1:1 – 11:32 103
2:1–25 30, 103
2:7 103
2:18 32, 33
2:23–25 33
2:25 30, 33
3:15 108
3:19 99, 103
6:17 95
12:1–3 128
12:2–3 127
27:29 119
37:10 119
41:43 119
45:22 13
49:8 119

Exodus
2:24 127
12:1–2 111
17:8 127
17:8–16 127
17:14 95, 126
17:16 119
34:6 69, 78

Leviticus
23:43 106
25:25–28 45, 51

Numbers
30:1–16 97
35:6–28 45

Deuteronomy
4:24 24
6:10–12 107
7:24 95
8:10–20 107
9:14 95
16:9 55
16:16 106
19:4–13 45
23:3–6 51, 54
23:13–17 106
23:21–23 97
25:5–10 51, 54
25:19 95
28 76
28:15–68 78
29:20 95
32:15 18

Joshua
2:8–9 123
7:1 127

Ruth
1:1 41, 42, 54
1:1–5 39
1:1–22 39, 44
1:2 54
1:6 40, 42, 54
1:7 41
1:8 41
1:8–9 43
1:10 41
1:11 41
1:11–13 43
1:12 41
1:12–15 41
1:13 42
1:16 41, 42
1:19–22 40
1:20 42
1:21 41, 42, 48
1:21–22 41
1:22 41, 43, 54
2:1 44, 46, 48
2:1–23 43, 46, 50
2:2 54
2:3 45
2:4 45, 48
2:6 54
2:9 44
2:10 44
2:12 44, 47

2:13 44
2:16 44
2:18 50
2:20 45, 46, 47
2:21 54
2:22 44
3:1–18 46, 51
3:5 46
3:6 46
3:9 46
3:10 47
3:10–11 47
3:11 46, 48
3:12 47
3:14 47
3:15 48
3:17 48, 51
4:1 48
4:1–22 46, 48, 56, 135
4:3 54
4:5 54
4:10 54
4:11–12 49
4:13 49, 53
4:14–15 49
4:15 50
4:16–17 49
4:17 40, 49

1 Samuel
15:1–35 127
15:18 119
15:20–33 119

2 Samuel
1:27 62

1 Kings
4:32 30
11:3 27

2 Kings
14:27 95
23:26–27 77
25:1–21 59

Ezra
1:2 95
2:55 89
2:57 89
3:11 69
5:11 95
10:1–44 51

Nehemiah
1:1 117
1:4–5 95
2:1 117
13:1 54
13:23 54

Esther
1:1–9 115
1:1 – 2:23 114, 115, 117
1:1 – 8:17 118
1:2 117
1:10–20 119
1:19 114
2:5 117, 119
2:6 124, 126
2:8 120
2:8–18 118
2:10 114, 119
2:12–17 119
2:17 114
2:18 115
2:19–23 118
2:21–22 120
2:22–23 114
3:1 117, 119
3:1–15 114

3:1 – 9:19 115
3:4 119
3:7 121
3:8 130
3:10 117
3:15 115
4:1–3 121
4:1–17 116
4:12–14 122
4:14 114, 117, 123
4:15 122
4:15–16 121
4:16 119, 122, 123
4:17 120
5:1 129
5:1–8 115
5:13 117
6:1–2 114, 121
6:1–11 118
6:1–14 125
6:4 121
6:10 117
6:11 123
6:13 117, 123
7:1–9 115
7:1–10 114
7:6 117
7:8 121
8:1 117
8:1–17 114, 115, 118
8:7 117
8:9 127
8:11 115, 127
8:13 115
8:17 114, 115, 123, 127
9:1–19 115
9:1–32 116
9:1 – 10:3 114, 115

INDEX OF SCRIPTURE REFERENCES

9:10 117, 127
9:17–19 115
9:19 114
9:20–22 116
9:20–32 115
9:21 111
9:22 116, 122, 132
9:24 117
9:29 117
9:31 116, 117
10:1–3 115
10:3 25, 117

Job
42:1–5 65

Psalms
2:1–12 77
18 (title) 20
22:1 81
22:7 81
23:1–6 18
34:1–22 70
36:7 37
44:1–26 73
46:1–11 77
46:5 77
46:7 77
48:1–14 77
48:2 77
48:3 77
50:2 77
76:1–12 77
76:13 77
80:1–19 73
100:5 69
106:1 69
107:1 69
118:1–4 69
126:1–3 132
135:1–26 69

Proverbs
1:7 105
3:1–18 105
3:17 105
3:19–20 105
5:15–19 29
8:22–30 105
10:22 105
12:28 105
14:12 105
16:9 105
16:25 105
16:33 105, 125
31:1–31 53

Ecclesiastes
1:1 84, 86, 87, 89,
   91
1:1 – 4:16 96
1:2 85, 86, 87, 89,
   90, 91
1:3 91, 95
1:3 – 4:16 87, 91
1:4–11 85, 92, 95,
   98
1:8 101
1:9 95
1:12 84, 89, 92
1:13 93, 95, 103
1:14 95
1:15 101
1:16 93
1:17 91, 93
1:18 93, 101
2:1 84
2:1 – 3:22 96
2:3 93, 95
2:9 93
2:10 91
2:11 91, 95
2:12 93

2:13 93, 105
2:15–16 93
2:17 93, 95
2:18 91, 93, 95
2:19 86, 91, 93, 95
2:20 91, 93
2:21 91, 93
2:22 91, 95
2:22–23 93
2:23 91
2:24 85, 91
2:24–25 94
2:24–26 92
2:26 93
3:1 92, 95
3:1–8 92, 94
3:1–22 92, 99,
   103
3:1 – 4:6 92
3:9 91, 94
3:10 103
3:11 86, 94, 97,
   103, 104
3:13 85
3:14 94, 96
3:15 – 4:4 94
3:16 95
3:17 94, 102
3:18–21 94
3:20 95, 103
3:21–22 86
4:1 95
4:1–16 92
4:3 95
4:4–6 92
4:7 94
4:6 91
4:7–16 92, 94
4:8 91, 92
4:9 95
4:13–16 95

4:15 95
4:16 91, 95
4:17 (MT) 85, 86
4:17 – 5:8 (MT) 87
5:1 85, 86, 97, 98
5:1–7 98
5:1–9 87, 96
5:1–20 101, 103
5:2 95
5:6 96
5:7 87, 96
5:8–9 96
5:9 – 6:9 (MT) 87
5:10 – 6:9 87
5:18 85
6:1 84
6:9 85, 86
6:10–11 88
6:10 – 7:22 87
6:11 87
7:13 103, 105
7:14 99
7:23 103
7:23–29 87
7:27 84, 89, 90, 91
7:29 103
8:1–8 87
8:9 – 9:12 87
8:15 85
9:1 84
9:13 98
9:13 – 12:7 87
10:12 105
11:1–6 97
11:5 103
11:7 98
11:7–10 88, 99
11:9 99, 102
11:9 – 12:7 85
12:1 98, 101, 102
12:1–7 85, 97, 100

12:1–14 97, 98, 102
12:2 98, 99
12:2–5 99
12:2–6 98
12:3–4 99
12:4–5 99
12:5 99
12:6 98, 99, 100
12:7 99, 103
12:8 85, 86, 87, 89, 90, 99
12:9 84, 89, 100
12:9–10 100
12:9–11 101, 102
12:9–12 99
12:9–14 84, 86, 87, 99
12:10 89
12:11 101, 102, 135
12:11–12 100
12:12 100
12:12–14 102, 103
12:13 100, 105
12:13–14 100

Song of Songs
1:1 19, 22, 24
1:2 17
1:2 – 3:6 28
1:4 20
1:5–17 21
1:5 19, 21
1:6 27, 30
1:12 20
2:3 31
2:7 22
2:10 21
2:11–13 21
2:15 30

2:17 21
3:1 – 6:13 25
3:1 25
3:1–4 21
3:1–5 21
3:5 22
3:6 26
3:6–11 19, 26
3:7 – 5:1 28
3:11 19
4:1–7 21
4:6 21
4:8 – 5:1 30
4:12 – 5:1 31
5:2 – 6:1 28
5:2 – 6:3 21
5:2 25
5:7 26, 30
5:7–9 21
5:9–16 31
6:2 – 7:11 28
6:3 19
6:12 26
6:13 19
7:5 20
7:10 31
7:12 – 8:14 28
8:2 23
8:4 22
8:5 23, 24, 25, 26, 31
8:5–7 23
8:6 23, 24, 26, 30
8:6–7 21, 23, 30
8:7 24
8:8–9 25, 30
8:8–14 25
8:10 25, 31, 33
8:11 19, 27
8:11–12 19, 27
8:12 27

INDEX OF SCRIPTURE REFERENCES

8:14 21, 34

Isaiah
1:29 18
5:1–7 28
14:12 62
14:12–23 66
40:1 63
40:2 63
66:24 69

Jeremiah
2:1–3 28
22:24 18
23:9–40 66
29:4–7 118
33:11 69
41:5 59

Lamentations
1:1 61, 73
1:1–11 62
1:3 73, 76
1:5 63, 64, 76
1:7 62, 73
1:8 63
1:9 62, 63, 76
1:11 62, 63
1:12 64
1:12–22 62
1:14 64
1:14–15 64
1:15 62, 64, 80
1:16 63, 66
1:17 62, 63, 64
1:18 63, 65
1:20 64
1:21 63
2:1 65, 66
2:1–17 66
2:1–22 65, 77

2:2 65
2:5 65
2:6 65, 66
2:7 65
2:13 66
2:14 66, 72
2:15 77, 80
2:15–16 81
2:17 65, 77
2:18–19 66
2:20 76, 78
2:20–22 66
2:21 65
2:22 65
3:1 67
3:1–16 67
3:1–18 67
3:1–39 67
3:1–66 60, 70
3:15 79
3:19–20 68
3:21 68
3:22–23 68, 74
3:24–27 70
3:24–39 69
3:27 70
3:39 67, 70
3:40–42 71
3:43–54 71
3:45 76, 80
3:46 71
3:51 71
3:54 71
3:62 71
3:64–66 71
4:1–20 72
4:1–22 77
4:2 72
4:4 72
4:5 72
4:6 72

4:7–8 72
4:10 72, 76
4:12 77
4:13 72
4:13–15 72
4:16 76
4:17 73
4:17–20 72
4:20 72, 77
4:21–22 72
5:1 74
5:1–22 60
5:2–3 73
5:2–18 74
5:4 73
5:5 73
5:7 74
5:9 73
5:12 76
5:13 73
5:16 74
5:18 73
5:19 74
5:20 77
5:20–21 74
5:21 73, 74
5:22 75

Ezekiel
1:2 126
16:8 46

Daniel
1:1 – 6:28 118
1:8 120
2:18–19 95
3:1–30 119

Hosea
2:14 28
11:1 35

11:8 35

Micah
1:19 18
6:8 55

Zechariah
7:3 59
7:5 59
8:19 59

Malachi
4:5–6 81

Matthew
1:1 56
1:1–17 135
1:3 56
1:5 56
1:6 56
2:1–12 56
4:12–17 56
5:11 131
8:20 33
19:5–6 33
19:12 33
22:30 34
28:18 57

Mark
10:8 33
15:20–39 80
15:29–30 80, 81

Luke
9:24 33
9:58 33
14:33 33
20:35 34
24:45–47 81

John
3:16 35
17:14 132

Acts
8:23 79
17:31 108

Romans
2:8 81
5:6–9 81
8:12–17 108
8:19–24 107
8:28 57, 131
9:1–5 81
11:1–24 81

1 Corinthians
4:13 79
6:16 33
7:1–40 33
13:12 83
15:1–58 33
15:35–49 33
16:10 108

2 Corinthians
7:8–11 79
15:58 108

Galatians
2:20 35
3:15–22 130
5:22 57

Ephesians
2:3–7 81
2:7 56
2:11–22 131
4:32 57
5:2 35

5:25 35
5:31 33
5:31–32 34

Philippians
2:30 108

1 Thessalonians
1:10 81

2 Thessalonians
1:5–10 81

2 Timothy
1:10 108

Titus
3:4 56

Hebrews
13:4 33

1 Peter
1:1 131
1:22 35
2:3–17 131

1 John
1:8–9 81

Revelation
14:20 80
17:14 22
18:20 132
19:6–10 34
19:15 80
19:16 22
21:1 – 22:5 81
22:17 34
22:20 34

Index of ancient sources

JEWISH LITERATURE
2 Maccabees 109
4 Esdras 52
Josephus
  Against Apion
    1.8 52
    1.42 13
  Antiquities
    5.9.2 40
Judith 112
Jubilees
  1:1 55
  4:17 56
Tobit 112

RABBINIC LITERATURE
Babylonian Talmud
  Megilloth **7a** 126
  Pesaḥîm **68b** 55
Jerusalem Talmud
  Megilloth **70d** 126
Midrash
  Tanḥuma 55

Ruth Rabbah 2:10 54
Mishnah 124
Mishnah *Yadaim*
  3.5 28
Targum to the Song of Songs 28

PATRISTICS
Clement of Alexandria
  Paedagogue 3.12.5 129, 130
Clement of Rome
  1 Clement **55** 128
Hippolytus 128
Miletus 129
Origen
  Commentary on
  Pss. 1 – 25 129

CLASSICAL LITERATURE
Herodotus
  The Histories
    96–97, 485 119